A HERMENEUTICS
OF ULTIMACY:
PERIL OR PROMISE?

CONTRIBUTORS

James H. Olthuis is Professor of Philosophical Theology at the Institute for Christian Studies, Toronto, Ontario

Clark H. Pinnock is Professor of Systematic Theology at McMaster Divinity College, Hamilton, Ontario

Donald G. Bloesch is Professor of Theology at the University of Dubuque Theological Seminary, Dubuque, Iowa

Gerald T. Sheppard is Professor of Old Testament at Emmanuel College of the University of Toronto, Toronto, Ontario

A HERMENEUTICS OF ULTIMACY: PERIL OR PROMISE?

James H. Olthuis

with Donald G. Bloesch,
Clark H. Pinnock and
Gerald T. Sheppard

UNIVERSITY
PRESS OF
AMERICA

LANHAM/NEW YORK/LONDON

Copyright © 1987 by

University Press of America,® Inc.

4720 Boston Way
Lanham, MD 20706

3 Henrietta Street
London WC2E 8LU England

Printed in the United States of America

British Cataloging in Publication Information Available

Co-published by arrangement with the
Institute for Christian Studies, Toronto, Ontario, Canada

Cover/book design & typography: Willem Hart

Library of Congress Cataloging in Publication Data

Olthuis, James H.
   A hermeneutics of ultimacy.

   (Christian studies today)
   Bibliography: p.
   1. Bible—Hermeneutics.   2. Evangelicalism.
I. Title.   II. Series.
BS476.054   1987   220.6'01   86-28071
ISBN 0-8191-5800-3 (alk paper)
ISBN 0-8191-5801-1 (pbk. : alk. paper)

All University Press of America books are produced on acid-free
paper which exceeds the minimum standards set by the National
Historical Publication and Records Commission.

TABLE OF CONTENTS

Though a man had a precious and a rich jewel, yet if he knew not the value thereof, nor wherefore it served, he were neither the better nor richer of a straw. Even so though we read the scripture, and babble of it ever so much, yet if we know not the use of it, and wherefore it was given, and what is therein to be sought, it profits us nothing at all. It is not enough, therefore, to read and talk of it only, but we must also desire God, day and night, instantly, to open our eyes, and to make us understand and feel wherefore the scripture was given, that we may apply the medicine of the scripture, every man to his own sores. Unless we intend to be idle disputers, and brawlers about vain words, ever gnawing upon the bitter bark without, and never attaining unto the sweet pith within; and persecuting one another in defending of wicked imaginations, and phantasies of our own invention.

William Tyndale
prefixed to the translation of the Pentateuch, 1530

Thus one who knows how to use the Scriptures properly, is in want of nothing for salvation, or for a holy life.

John Calvin
Commentary on II Timothy 3:16, **1548**

Foreword

It is perhaps a healthy sign that in our day the Bible has become a controversial book. Even the worst heresies at least have the merit of arousing the faithful to a renewed interest in the Word of God by which they claim to live. The focus of attention today revolves about the method of interpreting Scripture, called hermeneutics. Even those who hold, as I do, that Scripture is self-authenticating have to acknowledge that the text of Scripture nevertheless needs to be expounded and related to the world of meaning of our time.

The hermeneutics debate initiated by the "new hermeneutic" of Ebeling and Fuchs has only recently penetrated into evangelical circles. Now that the historical investigation of Scripture is becoming more generally accepted, evangelicals are increasingly entering into the dialogue on biblical interpretation.

James Olthuis' essay, together with my response and that of Clark Pinnock, were papers originally presented in June, 1981, at a conference in Toronto called "Interpreting an Authoritative Scripture," co-sponsored by the Institute for Christian Studies and Fuller Theological Seminary. Olthuis has enlarged his essay for this book and has composed a reply to his critics. We have also invited Gerald Sheppard, an active participant at the conference, to write a response for inclusion in this volume. We believe these papers are important because they show evangelicals wrestling with the basic issues of biblical interpretation raised by the later Heidegger, Gadamer and the New Hermeneutic.

The current debate on hermeneutics revolves around a number of issues, most of which are discussed in these papers. The first has to do with the meaning of hermeneutics. It is now generally agreed that hermeneutics is concerned not only with the understanding of the text in question but also with the meaning of "understanding" itself. There is a growing consensus that the aim of hermeneutics is not simply the reconstruction of the historical and literary background of a text but the translation of the meaning of the text into the thought world of the modern age. It is

an attempt to fuse the horizons of the original authors and the contemporary interpreters (Gadamer). Hermeneutic philosophers today speak of the need for a hermeneutical bridge that will span
the distance between the modern and ancient world views.

A closely related question concerns the focus of hermeneutics.
Is the biblical interpreter concerned most of all to gain a knowledge of authorial intention (the prevailing evangelical stance
today), authorial motivation (Schleiermacher), the inner life of
the author (Dilthey), authentic existence in the light of the text
(Bultmann) or the disclosure of Being through the text (Heidegger)? James Olthuis presents a fresh alternative in his conception of the vision of the text, an approach which purportedly
gives greater significance to the revelation of God in biblical
history.

In this same connection, we must ask: Is the criterion for
determining the truth of the text the inner disposition of the
author, the modern cultural experience of a holistic humanity, the
horizon of meaning entertained by the author or a fresh Word
from God who enters into the hermeneutical circle from the beyond
and reshapes our attitudes and presuppositions? This last is
Barth's position.

The role of a preunderstanding is also important in this
discussion. Drawing upon Heidegger and Gadamer, the new hermeneutic theologians contend that one cannot rightly understand
the meaning of the text unless one already shares in this meaning
to some extent. We cannot understand unless we are in the hermeneutical circle, which presupposes a preunderstanding of the
text. Tillich and Bultmann have said that we must come to the
text with the tools of existentialist analysis.   Karl Barth in
contrast has argued that we must come to the Bible laying aside
all overt presuppositions as much as possible and let the Bible
speak for itself. When we do this, the living Word of God acting
in the Bible corrects our preconceptions and places our broken understanding on a new foundation.

This brings us to the relation between biblical interpretation
and philosophical understanding. Olthuis builds his hermeneutic
partly on the basis of insights drawn from Dooyeweerd, the Dutch
Calvinist philosopher, as well as modern existentialists (Heidegger, Gadamer, Fuchs, Ebeling, Ricoeur).* Barth on the other
hand maintains that philosophical concepts can only be tools for
clarification in the hands of the theologian, not criteria for determining the adequacy of the hermeneutical enterprise. In Barth's
view, biblical hermeneutics must not be constructed in the

light of a general or philosophical hermeneutic but instead must draw its principles of interpretation from revelation itself.

No discussion of biblical hermeneutics can afford to ignore the meaning of revelation. Evangelical theology in the Reformation tradition has steadfastly maintained that revelation consists in an objective propositional content that resides in Holy Scripture but is accessible to us only by the illumination of the Holy Spirit. Some evangelical theologians (such as Carl Henry and Gordon Clark) claim that the datum of revelation can be apprehended by natural reason alone but that the illumination of the Spirit is necessary for the commitment of faith in the object of this revelation — Jesus Christ. This is also Pannenberg's position. Existentialist theology generally maintains that revelation gives us not conceptual knowledge of God and of his will and purpose but instead a new self-understanding. All contributors to this symposium contend for a conceptual or propositional dimension to revelation.

We must also consider whether the biblical symbols render real knowledge of God and the self or only a "true awareness" (Tillich). Paul Ricoeur concludes that the biblical symbols are equivocal rather than univocal, that is to say they contain a multiplicity of meanings. Their meanings are not absolute but relative — depending on the culture and history in which they were written and in which they are interpreted. Do the symbols point beyond themselves to an ineffable experience of the unconditional or Being-itself (as in mysticism), to a breakthrough into a higher level of consciousness (as in modern evolutionary theology), or do they adequately convey the conceptual truth that God intends us to hear concerning his promises and commandments? Is our knowledge of God basically symbolic in the sense of intuitive, or is it not analogical — giving us a real but limited understanding of the being and purpose of God?

Finally, we need to ask what are the limits of the historical investigation of Scripture. Is there a place for higher as well as lower (textual) criticism? Does the investigation of the historical background and linguistic history of the text support or subvert the claims of faith? Is it permissible to examine the historical and cultural context of the text but impermissible to critique the message of the text in the light of modern experience (*Sachkritik*)? Existentialist theologians make a real place of *Sache* (content) criticism whereas Barthians vigorously reject it. In Barth's view (which I share) the modern cultural experience must be critiqued in the light of Scripture and not vice versa.

While acknowledging that all Scripture texts participate in the relativity of history and the limitations of culture, we contend as evangelicals that every text is at the same time historically and culturally transcendent in that what it witnesses to is the living Word of God that enters into history and culture from the beyond. This Word which we find present though hidden in Scripture enables us to judge both the validity of historical and cultural norms and the authenticity of the church's witness throughout history. Historical and literary criticism have their place in throwing light upon the historical and cultural background of the text, but they cannot procure for us the Word of God — the Christological significance of every text which cannot be fully known until it is personally or existentially appropriated.

I believe that the discussion in this book throws light on most of these issues and should promote an interest among evangelicals in this ongoing debate in theology and biblical studies. It is a controversy that directly concerns biblical authority and the role of the Bible in the church's proclamation. Can the discipline of hermeneutics enable us to reappropriate biblical authority for our time, or does it signify the eclipse of biblical authority in the modern age? The answer to this question will probably not be decided until the evangelical contribution begins to make an impact on the wider academic community.

Donald G. Bloesch

---

* *I grant that such scholars as Gadamer and Ricoeur have been critical of certain thrusts in existentialism, but they nevertheless remain within this general orientation.*

Proposal for a hermeneutics of ultimacy

by James H. Olthuis

The nature, structure, and function of biblical authority remain of crucial importance to the Christian Church. If we do not believe in Jesus Christ according to the Scriptures, we cannot claim to be Christian. To be Christian means to hear the voice of God in the words of Scripture and to bow before it in faith. To receive the Bible as revealing the Word of God and to submit oneself to the Word in faith is the crux of accepting biblical authority. All Christians are one on this fundamental issue.

But, as James Packer frankly states, "Biblical authority is an empty notion unless we know how to determine what the Bible means."[1] And on that issue we are far from one. In fact, we are not even one in our understanding, confessing and conceptualizing of our most fundamental agreements. We interpret Scripture in a variety of ways and often with conflicting results. Moreover, we differ widely on how we are to live out its authority in our daily lives.

If this essay helps us make a little more headway in sorting out the issues involved in interpreting Scripture, I will be delighted. I intend to approach the issues in the context of the ongoing contemporary discussions in hermeneutics. My comments will be largely methodological and philosophic in nature, first in regard to scriptural authority and then in regard to interpretation of Scripture.

Views of scriptural authority distinct from authority itself
In the Christian Church, we have different views of biblical authority. That is the reality. What is also real is the ever-present danger that we declare all those whose concepts of biblical authority are not the same as ours to be heretics, infidels, and hypocrites, or at the very least, underminers of biblical authority. The danger is seductive because our submission to the Scriptures as the Word of God never takes place apart from concrete embodiment in a view of biblical authority through which and in which we articulate our submission. The existential surrender to the God of the Scriptures is always embedded in the

historical process: it happened here, at this time, in this community, through this particular vision of biblical authority. It is
in terms of the language and symbolism of a certain tradition that
the submission to God and the Word of God takes place.

Not only do we surrender to the Scriptures in terms of a
culturally conditioned vision of life, including a doctrine of Scripture; we also need to express our basic submission to Scripture in
terms of a particular conception of what Scripture is if we wish to
communicate and perpetuate our submission. Indeed, we can be true
to ourselves and to our confession only from within a tradition and
by being faithful to it.

At the same time, the fact that our confession of biblical
authority takes place in terms of a particular tradition ought to
remind us that the particular way we confess submission to the
Scriptures is not simply the product of faith; it is also the
articulation of faith in interaction with the kinds of persons we
are, the conceptual frameworks in which we work, the kinds of
communities and the historical times in which we live. That
reality, once accepted, brings a necessary distinction to the fore,
and with the distinction a relativity, and with the relativity,
humility.   We need to distinguish our in-faith-acceptance of the
Scriptures from the way we conceptualize and articulate it. If we
acknowledge that both our conceptualizations and the tradition in
terms of which we articulate our fundamental acceptance of the
Scriptures are time-conditioned and subject to human fallibility,
we will be able to be open to other confessions of biblical
authority. We will be enabled to relativize our own views of biblical authority without relativizing our acceptance of the Scriptures as God's Word for Life.

Practising what Paul Ricoeur has called a hermeneutics of
suspicion[2] on our own views, we will be able to resist the temptation to canonize our views about the canon and will be able to
honor and learn from other traditions. The avenues of communication will remain open, and as brothers and sisters in Christ we
will struggle with each other humbly and respectfully in the
communion of love.

Conceptual systems and the ultimate
In our day to day experience we make sense of reality by
integrating the various givens into wholes or gestalts in terms of a
categorial framework. The perception of any reality requires
working within and thus accepting a particular framework. As
Polanyi would explain it: focal awareness of data depends on

tacit reliance on a conceptual system.[3] The conceptual systems themselves are tacitly experienced as valid because we find that we are able to cope adequately with human experience using them.

In experiencing a conceptual system as valid, we also tacitly experience our reliance on the ultimate which is the ground on which the system rests. It is our dependence on this ultimate which makes comprehension possible. Any cognition of a particular thing occurs in a framework whose ultimate horizon is the reality of this ultimate.

However, since conceptual systems are grounded in the ultimate, they provide a narrower frame of reference than the ultimate itself. This in turn means, as Polanyi has argued at length, that we can only know the ultimate tacitly and never through focal comprehension. We never have a cognitive knowledge of the ultimate in the sense of comprehending an entity in the light of some framework. Our frameworks, in terms of which we make sense of the world, cannot legitimately and univocally be extrapolated and employed to comprehend the ultimate.

Moreover, although from the structure of cognitive knowing it is demonstrable that an ultimate horizon with its ultimate is necessary, such demonstration falls short of establishing who or what the ultimate is. In fact, as does happen, the ultimate could be No-thing, ultimate meaninglessness. None of this makes the knowledge of the ultimate any less real in the experience of the knower. It does point to the unique nature of such knowledge: this knowledge is revelation accepted in the surrender of faith.

How is it revelation? The ultimate cognitive impotence of humanity to comprehend the ultimate means that such knowledge of the ultimate is received as a gift — that is, as revelation. In Gilkey's words, revelation "...is that definite mode of experience in which a particular answer to these ultimate questions that arise in relation to all secular life manifests itself, is received, and so 'known'....Revelation so defined is universal in human existence."[4] Since human powers of cognition are grounded in the ultimate and are ordered and directed towards the ultimate, such manifestations or revelations of the ultimate can be received and recognized by humans only in faith.

Wittgenstein also concludes that every thinker necessarily comes to an end point where he takes a final stand which can no longer be justified by a series of arguments. "If I have exhausted the justifications, I have reached bedrock, and my spade is turned. Then I am inclined to say: 'This is simply what I do.'"[5] In his last

writing, *On Certainty*, he pursued the theme.[6] Certain propositions "lie apart from the route travelled by inquiry;" they are
"fixed...removed from traffic...so to speak shunted onto an unused
siding." They give us "our way of looking at things;" they provide
the "*scaffolding* of our thoughts." They are the "hinges" which
"stay put" and on which our everyday propositions turn.

Every thinker necessarily begins with some faith intuition
received as revelation: as I have learned from my colleague Hendrik Hart,[7] this is also the far-ranging conclusion which follows
from Gödel's incompleteness theorem (in any formal system there
is always an element of its proof that is not itself provable in the
theory). Oxford mathematician Morris Kline discusses the
implications of this theorem for the field of mathematics which
has long been and still is considered an area where ultimate, universally accepted proof is possible, and he concludes: "Apparently the price of consistency is incompleteness." Kline points out
that "mathematicians have been worshipping a golden calf —
rigorous, universally accepted proof, true in all possible worlds —
in the belief that it was God. They now realize it was a false
god."[8]

Authority and evidence
These recent explanations of the foundational role of faith
commitment in human cognition support my view that scriptural
authority is self-authenticating, worked in a person's heart by
the testimony of the Holy Spirit. In other words, I do not believe
that we accept the authority of the Bible at bottom because of or
on account of the empirical evidence of Christian experience (J.
Oliver Buswell, Jr.), nor moral value evidence (E. J. Carnell), nor
historical evidence (John Warwick Montgomery and Clark
Pinnock), nor the rationality of Christian truth (Carl F. H. Henry
and Gordon Clark).

This is not to say that there is no evidence for the authority
of the Bible or even that its authority cannot be inferred from such
evidence. I believe, in fact, that there is such evidence, and of all
the kinds mentioned. But I am not persuaded that we ultimately
affirm scriptural authority on the basis of such evidence. We may
have reasons for so affirming. Such reasons certainly help bolster
our confession. But although the presenting of reasons plays a
necessary and constructive role, reasons can never serve as the
final basis and ground for faith in God and in the authority of
Scripture. Final justification of ultimate faith — and faith in
Scripture is such an ultimate matter — is a unique kind of

justification.

What I am saying amounts to this: in the final analysis, when everything else is said and done, we do not accept the Bible to be the Normative Guide for our lives, the Word of God, by rational persuasion. Such fundamental acceptance does not come *from* reasons, although it may come *through* reasons. At the same time, our entrustment necessarily gives rise to reasons and a view of authority which articulates its own reasons. Once we attest to the Bible's authority, we confess that its trustworthiness is accounted for and explained because it is the Word of God.

However, even though the ultimate entrustment of ourselves to the God revealed in Jesus Christ and to the Scriptures of God is not based on reasons, we must be careful not to call such entrusting in any sense "irrational." To call it "irrational" would be to suggest that there is another way to start, as if to begin with entrusting is contrary to the principles of human reasoning. But that is not the case. The need to begin with a given received in faith, a revelation, is no restriction on human knowing. In fact, faith commitment is the very condition through which human cognition reveals its intelligibility. As we have noted, the fact that every thinker necessarily begins with some faith intuition as to what is ultimately trustworthy and real is one of the great discoveries of modern thought. The primary religious commitment of faith is not to be described either as a "reasoned conclusion or an unreasoned hunch."[9]

In the commitment of faith, basic beliefs are received as revelation. These basic beliefs of faith, organized and fit together in a worldview, provide us with ways of seeing things and of structuring our experience which are prior to any conceptualization of it. They are the basic beliefs from which our rational judgments begin, founding our relations of inquiry into the actual. No vision or view of reality, including our view of the Scriptures, is subject to proof in the sense that we can derive its basic principles from a process of thought prior to them. The core affirmations which found and ground our living in the world are received as revelation and thus known as truth. Standing in them, dwelling in them, to adopt Polanyi's phrase, is their final and culminating validation.

It is in the faith dimension (or as I shall term it later, the "certitudinal" mode, or, as is becoming more common, the "ultimacy" dimension) of human experience that answers to ultimate questions are received as revelation. To experience the dimension of ultimacy in our knowing and doing is to recognize that the ultimate basis for our knowledge will be for us self-evident. For the ultimate to which we surrender is the ground for our lives, the ground which requires no other ground, the ground of and for all other grounds. This ground will, by the nature of the structural dynamics of human knowing, be experienced as self-evident or, as Calvin put it in reference to Scripture, "self-authenticating."[10] That is to say, as we commit ourselves to the ultimate, the ultimate functions for us as its own evidence for ultimacy. If we accept the ultimate on the basis of some other ground, this ground is in fact our final ground, our true ultimate, as Gilkey argues, our true "high" god.[11] The ultimate cannot be proven. If it is, it contradicts its own intention to be Final.

I am saying that our faith leads our cognitive knowing. At the same time, our cognitive knowing provides the foundational structure, by laying out the possibilities for faith. We are dealing with a two-directional process. Although our faith in the last analysis is not dependent on our cognitive knowing (it is received as a gift of revelation), and we do not in the last analysis entrust ourselves to the ultimate on the basis of rational reasons, that does not mean that our faith has no reasons and is irrational. Moreover, since we exercise and confess our faith in terms of a vision of life, a vision of life which we can rationally explain and defend, rational argument has its place. Such argumentation can even be the basis on which a person adopts a new worldview — provided, I suggest, that the underlying faith commitment with its core beliefs remains the same. Thus Christians may move from an ascetic withdrawal-from-culture worldview to a more accommodating Christ-and-culture vision, from a nature-grace Thomism to a Christ-transforms-culture worldview.

However, since the core beliefs intrinsic to a vision of life are received as revelation, rational argumentation can only be the *means* by which but not the *ground* on which a person accepts a new faith. Rational argument may occasion a change of faith, and may, in a fundamental way, urge the invalidity of a vision and its underlying faith. But in the end, such faith crises are resolved through conversion to a new faith which reaches far beyond rational demonstration and logical proof.

Understanding as gift and call
Our fundamental acceptance of the Scriptures as the authoritative speaking of God guides our interpretation of Scripture. The Word-Spirit of God knows us first; then we interpret God's Word in its meaning for our lives. In the historical process, of

course, God's gracious initiative occurs simultaneously in, through, and under all our human searching, hearing and reading of God's Word in Scripture. Consequently, "first" is not to be read as chronologically first in an arithmetic series, but in the sense of "fundamentally," "ultimately."

In the Spirit we are gifted with understanding and called to understanding. The gift and call belong together as two sides of the same coin. The gift is a constant call to understand anew what Scripture means for us today. The gift of understanding needs to be properly accepted, appropriated and filled in if the Power of Word and Spirit is to transform our lives. Working out our salvation with fear and trembling includes the work of interpretation, discerning the good and acceptable Will of God, for it is God that works in us (cf. Phil. 2:12-13; Romans 12:2).

Understanding the Scripture as the Canon for the new creation is in principle a gift (*Gabe*) of the Spirit which calls us to interpretation as a task (*Aufgabe*). If that is true, exegetes bear an impossible burden when they are mandated to determine whether or not Scripture bears the Authority of God, and interpretation is made too difficult. In fact, I think that the current crisis in biblical scholarship revolves around the suspicion that no amount of scientific-historical critique can decide the basic question of scriptural authority.

Textual criticism is delivering a more accurate text. Philological-grammatical study is increasing our understanding of the forms, syntax, and significance of language. Historical criticism has made us extremely sensitive to the *Sitz im Leben* of language. Literary source criticism has alerted us to the rhetorical, poetic, and compositional devices employed. Form criticism has made us aware of the place of (oral) units of material in relation to earlier life of a community. Redaction criticism has introduced us to final writers who composed literary works on the basis of various sources. But all this has not resulted in significant agreement in interpretation of the biblical text or on its status as Canon.

On the other hand, many in the Evangelical Church make interpretation too simple. They have shied away from hermeneutic concerns, conveniently assuming, it would seem, that whereas others "interpret" (that is, mishandle and dismantle) the Scriptures, they simply "read" (that is, rightly understand) the Scriptures. The problem here is insufficient realization of the fact that readers of Scripture employ methods of human construction and human fallibility. Not only that, but such readers have too often proceeded as if their view of the authority of Scripture were identical with scriptural authority itself. When that is presumed to be the case, any view which does not agree with theirs is *ipso facto* unbiblical.

I have already emphasized the necessity of distinguishing views about scriptural authority from the authority itself. I have also pointed to the crucial nature of these views because it is through them that scriptural authority is either honored or obscured. The view functions as the lens, funnel, or filter through which biblical authority works itself out in our lives. Our view of biblical authority, along with a number of other core beliefs about who God is, who we are, where we are going, and what our task is, forms a vision of life which is the "spectacles" through which we make sense of life. The vision is a pattern of reciprocally related beliefs which act as the integrative and interpretive framework for life.

David Kelsey in his important book, *The Uses of Scripture in Recent Theology,* makes a similar point in a somewhat different way. He talks of the "imaginative judgement" which provides a vision of scriptural normativity (he talks of the *discrimen*) for judging and shaping theological proposals.[12] He has drawn Evangelical fire, I think rightly, because he concludes that Scripture cannot serve as a final court of appeal because of the many visions of scriptural authority. But we need to take more seriously than we do the reality and importance of the plurality of such visions. Although the normativity of the Scriptures is not finally grounded in life in the church as Kelsey suggests, the Scriptures are experienced as normative in terms of the *discrimen* or vision which does emerge in the church. No group, not even Evangelicals, may assume that their view is automatically the only biblical view of authority.

The importance of all of this for interpretation ought to be obvious. We have access to Scripture and refer to Scripture only in terms of our vision of what Scripture is and how it norms life. The results of close exegetical study of the biblical text can be decisive only to members of the same tradition, operating with the same vision, looking through the same "spectacles." The center of gravity in theological circles needs to shift from a narrow concern with biblical passages and their backgrounds to a broader discussion of the visions in terms of which the exegesis makes sense. Until that happens we will continue to be frustrated by our exegetical disagreements.

Any conception of biblical authority is validated to the degree that it empowers Christians to experience the Bible as useful for teaching the faith and for resetting the direction of our lives, as the comprehensive equipment fitting us fully for all branches of work (II Timothy 3:16 and 17). It is through experiencing it that scriptural authority takes on meaning as canonic direction for life. In that basic sense every view of authority needs to be "functional."

To experience biblical authority, we need to know what the Bible says. What the Bible says becomes clear in human interpretation. Therefore, a high view of Scripture commits us to full involvement in all matters of interpretation and to hermeneutics as the theory of interpretation. In what follows I state and explicate six theses as central to my developing hermeneutic.

Interpretration and mis-interpretation

1. Every text needs interpretation in order to be understood. Only when there is a breakdown in communication, which can be caused by the intrusion of any of a host of factors, does interpretation become problematic and demand special attention.

Interpretation is a fact of human life. We are always interpreting, not just when reading books, but when looking at pictures, observing signs, or listening to music. We interpret a row of books to be an indication of a library; a wedding-band signifies that its bearer is married; a red light is a signal to stop. Most often we pay little attention to the interpretive moment; it happens more or less automatically in the pull and press of ordinary life.

There are other facets of interpretation. We are motivated by a desire to learn and share in relation with others. Sometimes interpretation leads to communion, to sharing the inner thoughts and lives of other persons. Moreover, how much enthusiasm we bring to interpreting depends largely on how much significance the event, person or subject matter has for us.

It is only when there is a breakdown in communication that we give special attention to interpretation and mis-interpretation. The row of books could mean a bookstore; the wedding-band may be a decoy to avoid involvement; the light could be stuck on red. There are countless situations of this kind: not clearly hearing the phonemes, being unable to decipher handwriting, meeting strange words or puzzling word combinations, not wanting to hear or being unable to hear due to some emotional block. And we all know that such mis-interpretations take place with frustrating regularity between people speaking the same language, living under the same roof, in the same community, even when they have the advantage of accompanying gestures, tonal inflection, facial expression, and emotional fervor.

The more or less automatic way we interpret in the practice of daily living, as well as the numerous breakdowns in communication which we experience, have special meaning with reference to the interpretation of written texts. In the first place, since a text is a semantic objectification of subjective meaning intention, a human being must read and interpret the text in order for its meaning to be unlocked. If one has acquired the ability to decode and the text is in a familiar language and script, such reading can be relatively easy and straightforward. Little attention needs to be paid to the syntax or words. The language is relatively clear. One can concentrate on the meaning of the discourse.

However, such free-flowing interpretation becomes difficult and jerky when the reader lacks familiarity with the subject matter or is predisposed against the message of the text or approaches the text with faulty expectations. Then, even though the words are themselves familiar, reading becomes laborious, frustrating and difficult. Mis-interpretation or fanciful exegesis — in biblical hermeneutics often called eisegesis — becomes a very real possibility. The more dense, complex, or allusive the text, the more complicated the process of interpretation. If, in addition, the text is written in an unfamiliar literary form, or if its author hails from another culture and another time, interpretation is that much more difficult. If the text is written in a strange language, interpretation cannot, of course, begin until the text is translated, no small feat of interpretation in itself.

There is a wide variety of extra-lingual features which often serve to obfuscate and hinder proper interpretation. Removing the philological, syntactical and semantic hindrances no doubt helps interpretation. However, when the words are decoded and the syntax cleared up, the meaning may be even more unclear. Differing perspectives on life, emotional blockages, political allegiances, socio-economic conditions — all can function to open up or close down proper interpretation.

Proper interpretation is an art to be learned and practised, a complex conversation between interpreter and text in which the meaning-world of the text is elucidated for the enlargement of the interpreter's world. We can be greatly helped in these conversations by experts of many kinds. Hermeneutics — the theoretic science which studies and explains the structural principles involved in the art of interpretation — can be an invaluable help toward an adequate and illuminating exegesis.

Interpretation of Scripture

On a first, basic level the Scriptures are most clear: Believe on the Lord Jesus Christ and be saved to new life by the Word and Spirit of God! Work out your healing with fear and trembling wherever you are placed, for the God who saves and empowers you is the faithful God who made you and will never forsake you! There is one message; at the same time, the Scriptures are a collection of books (*biblia*) of varying literary forms written by various authors and editors, in specific languages, in historically diverse times of the past, in varied geographical contexts, in varied cultural settings and in response to a wide range of situations and needs. And along with the textual complexity, there is in Scripture a dynamic unfolding, recontextualizing and deepening of thematic content. The meaning spirals back and forth, contracting and expanding.

On the one hand, the clarity of the basic message of Scripture makes clear that its interpretation on a fundamental level is not a technical matter reserved for experts, be they theologians, linguists, or philosophers. The fundamental interpretation is a pre-theoretic act of listening and responding, open to all people. Indeed, countless generations of Christians have learned the art of reading the Scriptures and have been daily nourished in their faith in so doing. Since, as we will soon discuss, the Bible is a faith-focused book, exegesis of Scripture is first and foremost an activity of faith and not of reason, passion or science.

On the other hand, the complexity and diversity of the scriptural documents in form, style, language, and context, the development and recasting of their thematic content, and the traditions, worldviews, personal situations and prejudices which we bring to our reading all complicate the interpretive act. For these reasons the Scriptures require special attention before we can hear and do their message today. For many of us they even need to be translated into our native languages before we begin reading! Since the Bible is not only a book from another time and culture, but since the same host of factors which affect all our interpretive endeavors will also affect our exegesis of Scripture, we can be helped in our reading by experts. Scholars of all sorts and every stripe — historians, sociologists, linguists, ethicists, psychologists, theologians, philosophers, hermeneutists — have a contribution to make. Transposing and integrating such theoretic knowledge into our faith understanding, we can become more sensitive, highly tuned receivers of the Word of God clothed in human language.

Structural specificity of text

2. Proper identification of text-kind is heuristically indispensable to non-violation of the text.

Exposition of textual meaning begins with interpreting the semantic symbols. That is a minimal and foundational necessity. But it is not sufficient for interpretation. For, although meaning is mediated by words, it is not contained in their form. Words are symbols through which we open up (or obscure, as the case may be) the universe and our place in it. In their lingual meaning they refer beyond themselves to (non-semantic) reality. In other words, the meaning of a text, although presented in lingual discourse, is not linguistically determinable. Ebeling, Gadamer and the new hermeneutic have said it simply: we do not understand words; we understand through words.[13]

There is, of course, some definite correlation between linguistic form and textual meaning. But one linguistic form, as, for example, irony, can sponsor at least two different interpretations.[14] (For that matter, the same meaning can be represented by different linguistic forms; for example, "pants" and "trousers," "jacket" and "coat.")

Correct interpretation requires some awareness of the context or universe of discourse in which the linguistic discourse is meant. References to the appropriate context are built into a text structurally. Paul Ricoeur calls them the extra-linguistic referents which present the "world" of the text.

All texts find their structural specificity as a "kind" of text in the particular way of perceiving reality which their authors adopted in writing the text. Texts which take the political vantage point are known as politically qualified texts; texts which adopt the moral viewpoint are moral texts; and so on. Although all texts are foundationally lingual (being lingual is necessary to being text), texts are of different kinds (they bear differing structural qualifications). Texts are classified according to kind, according to the mode-of-being-in-the-world, adopted by their authors, that provides their over-riding or macro-purpose.

Awareness of structural specificity — how, or in what structural way, a text approaches what it is about — clues an interpreter into the universe of discourse, the form of life in which the text is at home. Since each way of being in the world has its own unique concerns, locating the structural way of perceiving the world which the author has adopted and codified in the text provides a set of criteria in reference to which the meaning-content of the text, its message or vision, can be understood. It is not enough for proper interpretation, I am saying, to know the subject matter treated in the text. What is crucial is knowledge about the angle of vision which the text takes: *how* it goes about what it is about. Thus, a political text can be about anything and everything. What qualifies it as a political text and not a psychological text or faith text is its political focus, in terms of which everything is discussed.

Respect for the kind of text is crucial if one is not to do violence to a text. Only when a text is read and judged in terms of the type and character of questions and concerns it sets out to address as a specific kind of text, do we honor the integrity of the text. When the particular text-kind is ignored, when a novel is read as a historical record, when a telephone book is taken to be a social registry, when a scientific text is taken to be a novel, there is no criterion (except one's own desires) to guide the interpretation. We need to determine, as Gadamer has stressed, the kinds of questions the text sets out to answer. Without attention to the structural qualification of a text, our questions run the risk not only of being inappropriate but of being illegitimate. Then we violate the text by forcing it into our mold, not allowing it to reveal itself in terms of its own intentionality or specificity. What asks to be heard — not what we wish to hear — has priority. A first step in understanding is standing-under the text in a manner appropriate to the nature of the text.

In interpretation there is no escape from identification of text-kind. The only question is whether we make such an identification consciously or unconsciously. Whenever we begin to interpret, we make some assumption as to the *kind* of text based on previous reading experience. This pre-judgment includes certain expectations concerning the whole of the text and triggers in our minds a relevant reading strategy. Proper identification of text-kind is necessary for good interpretation because a text is a whole, a totality. As Ricoeur has emphasized, it is "more than a linear sequence of sentences. It is a cumulative, holistic process."[15] No sentence, paragraph or chapter has a separate footing, nor are they separately understandable. The textual whole has a certain cast or flavor, with primary and subordinate topics, with central and peripheral sections, with crucial and supporting sentences. Interpreting any part of the text involves a presupposing of the text's architecture as a whole and, reciprocally, in construing the details we achieve a better sense of the whole.

Certitudinal texts

Identification of the text-kind of the Scriptures is indispensable if we are to develop a method of Scriptural interpretation which does justice to the text. Scripture, it is rightly said, must be interpreted according to its redemptive intention. That gives the full intent of the message of the Scripture. But it does not give the form. The form, of course, is a book, a collection of books that together compose the canonical text of the Scriptures. But it is a *specific kind* of book with a proper nature of its own.

In contrast to most other kinds of books, the Scriptures belong to a class of books which have as their governing focus the ultimate questions of life and death. These books, generally known as "sacred writings," deal with every sort of issue, but always from the viewpoint of ultimate certitude. Despite dissimilarity in literary genre, language, traditions, historical setting, sub-purposes, etc., such books have one overriding kind of preoccupation: calling to commitment, engendering faith, promoting hope, encouraging and exhorting certitude. Only when we approach sacred writings with an awareness of their overriding concern for life-certitude and ultimate healing are we able to do them justice.

Contemporary hermeneutics à la Gadamer tends to take all texts and all language to be this kind of fully opened-up oracular revelation of the being of reality. Gadamer treats every text as a certitudinal, sacred text. On the other hand, structuralism, at least in its pure form, seems the epitome of the opposite extreme, ignoring "language as disclosure, choice and actualization."[16] Although Gadamer skates on thin ice when he views every text as oracle, it is true that some texts have that character. The Scriptures certainly do.

The Scriptures are "certitudinal" in qualification, that is, their angle of perception is the certitudinal which can be "phenomenologically described as an ultimate or grounding dimension or horizon to all meaningful human activities."[17] It is by this dimension that we explicitly affirm or deny our relation to the Ultimate; we believe in or refuse to believe in God. All of us are creatures who seek certainty, search for final meaning, ultimate security and permanent bliss. Our believing-entrusting-faith way of being in the world (what I technically refer to as "certitudinal") not only functions to open up and ground life in ultimate certainty, it also integrates and guides life in terms of the ultimate ground.[18] Faith supplies a basic set of core beliefs which, organized in a vision of life, integrate and lead our daily walk of life. In this way, through its certitudinal qualification, the authority of Scripture can have and does have a scope as large as life itself.

Thus, for example, although Scripture is not as a whole a political tract, an economic treatise or a moral homily, it does fundamentally speak to our political, economic, and moral life out of and in terms of the ultimate horizon of faith. Even though Scripture is not a theoretic discourse or a book of science, it does speak to the scientific endeavor insofar as every theoretic conception and all scientific activity is grounded in and is an exposition of an ultimate commitment of faith.

The Scriptures are a classic example of a certitudinal text. First we come to them aware of their pervasive and compelling concern to edify us in the faith, to provide access in the Spirit to ultimate comfort, abiding hope and abundant healing; only then are we in the proper position to access the true intentions of the text as a single whole made up of an intriguing diversity of books. In this way we can find our way into the "world" of the text, allowing it to claim us and reshape our worlds. We will be empowered to hear the abiding message of Scripture as the speaking of the same God in historically dissimilar traditions and in a variety of literary genres. Approaching the text in this orientation — the faith orientation on certitude — we are attuned to Scripture, equipped to pick up its enduring and underlying message even as it comes in a variety of culturally-specific and time-bound expressions. We are, I suggest, better able to discern and follow the certitudinal "thread" — the abiding message — which is woven in and through the rich, multi-textured tapestry.

We have become increasingly sensitive to the diversity of literary genres in Scripture: parables need to be interpreted as parables, narrative as narrative, wisdom literature as wisdom literature, and so on. What we still need, in my view, is more conscious awareness of the presence of a broader, over-arching, all-encompassing "language-game" or form of life which characterizes the Bible *as a whole*; the language game of certitude. It was an overriding concern to generate and strengthen the certitudes of faith which guided authors, redactors and communities in the canonical process; awareness of that concern would help us immensely, not only to better understand the involved process of the re-contextualization of earlier meanings within the broader tradition, but also to understand how a particular text calls us to healing service in our time and culture.[19]

Interpretation of a certitudinal text is a matter of encounter and decision. We do not simply mine the text for its information. Rather, the text confronts us, and demands fundamental acceptance in order to be rightly and fully understood. Certitudinal texts are *par excellence* "encounter" or "surrender" texts that press an ultimate claim as the truth for life and death. The central message proclaimed asks for whole-hearted surrender, and so long as that does not happen, the text's salvific power to transform the self-understanding of the interpreter is limited. "Anyone who believes in the Son has eternal life, but anyone who refuses to believe in the Son will never see life: the anger of God stays on him or her" (John 3:36). Strictly speaking, to resist God's claim is to misunderstand the message. For if we really did understand, we would see it as the truth and change our lives accordingly — we would believe in the Son.

An open receptivity to the central claim of the biblical text puts us in a better position to understand the full text in depth and detail. That explains why interpreting certitudinal texts is excruciatingly difficult, if not in the end impossible, when the interpreter does not embrace the thrust of the text. Basic disagreement with or deep-seated resistance to the text's primary thrust is a very serious obstacle to its proper interpretation. On a most basic level the interpreter will be predisposed to skew the text. (At the same time, since understanding non-certitudinal texts does not depend so much on receptivity to the main message, we are also able to explain why such texts are more accessible to a fair and adequate reading even when they find their ultimate base in a faith at odds with the fundamental commitment of the reader.)

Although receptivity to the fundamental message greatly facilitates understanding, it certainly does not guarantee agreed-upon interpretations. We have already noted many of the factors which make exegesis an exceedingly complex and difficult affair. Indeed, all the great world religions have a variety of competing exegetical traditions. All of us are guided in our reading by our own prejudices, and we wear the interpretative glasses of our particular community. We are led, even tempted, to interpret a text in a manner which justifies our own positions. But now we are beginning to consider thesis three.

No neutral exegesis

3. Presuppositionless exegesis and methodically secured objectivity are illusions.

Modern hermeneutics has turned attention from the text to the

interpreter.[20] Schleiermacher, the father of modern hermeneutics, pointed out that a person may have all the grammatical-
historical insight required and still misunderstand the text. Since
Bultmann, theological exegetes have had to come face to face
with the fact that the pre-understanding (*Vorverständnis*) of the
interpreter dramatically affects and often determines the interpretation of the text. Presuppositionless or neutral exegesis is a
figment of the imagination.

Failure to be aware of one's fore-havings, fore-seeings and
fore-conceptions[21] leads to self-delusion. By strict adherence to
methodological procedures one can imagine acquiring an objective
interpretation free from all traces of subjectivity.[22] Proponents of
objectivity forget, however, that an interpreter can exist only in
terms of a specific tradition with all its trappings and prejudices.
It is ironic that such positivistic efforts which decry any ideology
exhibit the foremost feature of ideology: not being transparent to
self.

Methodically secured objectivity is, I suspect, an illusion. It
is a remarkable feature of our times that more and more people are
realizing that the foundational error involved in such efforts, re-
grettably endemic to modernity, is the acceptance of the
Cartesian/Kantian subject-object dualism. The Cartesian subject-
object split ("I am" over against the sense-perceivable world) has
denatured the interpretive process. In that framework one does
not begin from a desire to bring self into the proper mode of
relation to a text with the purpose of dialogue, sharing, and
communion. Rather, one begins with the observing consciousness as
the supreme arbiter of reality to which all things, including
Scripture, must give account; the text is simply a passive object to
be mastered. As follows from the Cartesian split, mastery, control, and exploitation describe the basic form of human engagement with the world. The subject-subject dialogue between an interpreter and an author who has objectified her meaning in a text
is reduced to an operation of a presupposition-less, body-less, a-
historical mind who determines the meaning of a passive object
through rigorous application of procedures in accordance with the
rules of exegesis. The movement is one way: from subject to object.

The problem is to get reliable knowledge, and the aim of
interpretation is to bring the world under rational control, the
measure of which control is its "objectivity." The human person —
rather, this disembodied consciousness — stands at the center of
the world as its foundation and judge. Since the 17th century, western thinkers have too often believed that the methods of human

subjectivity are the royal road to "objectivity." Understanding has been reduced to the acquisition of true propositions about the world of objects surrounding humankind. These root assumptions of modern thought have perverted interpretation.

But objectivity is a myth. The self-conscious ego of Descartes does not exist. In its splendid isolation it has been unmasked as an impossible abstraction, a false cognito.[23]

All thinkers are phenomenologically situated from the beginning in a context in terms of which they tacitly make sense of life. Every interpreter starts at a certain place, at some time, in a certain culture, with a vision of life and its received revelation as to the origin and basis of life. Interpreters are not disembodied, naked minds, but full-blooded persons whose thinking, interpreting, and acting reflect their emotional states, faith stances, politico-social conditions, etc.

The Cartesian mind is itself an invention of humankind, explicating a faith in the autonomy of human reason and in reason's capacity to achieve objective knowledge. No wonder that the historico-critical method is currently under attack, even from within its own ranks. As a legacy of the Enlightenment enthronement of Reason, it failed to take seriously the limitations and biases of the interpreter. (Evangelicals who tend to side with Betti and Hirsch in their debate with Gadamer do well to take more seriously that in the end, for Betti, it is the human operator, as the autonomous subject, who decides when objective meaning has been ascertained.) Not only do methods based on the Cartesian subject-object split neglect the subjective pre-understandings of the interpreter, they in fact violate the integrity of many texts by reducing them to books of information and deposits of propositional truth which are to be mined for reliable knowledge.

Openness to a text in the sense of submission to and respect for a text leading to encounter and dialogue have been alien to the scientistic tenor of modern thought. But it is pre-eminently with sacred texts that the direction of interpreter-to-text defeats the whole purpose of the text, which is to call into question one's world, to re-order and renew it.

The hermeneutic spiral

4. Interpretation is a dialogic process of hermeneutic spiral between interpreter (and his/her vision of life) and the text (and its implied vision).

To talk of interpretation as dialogue and decision is to be talking of a hermeneutic spiral between text and interpreter.

Interpreters ask questions of the text from their own situatedness. The answers of the text affect, question, and subtly change our being in the world. The next round of questions put by the interpreters in answer to the text's claims is consequently somewhat different — as are the answers and the implicit questions provided by the text.

In the process more and more hidden assumptions reveal themselves and become explicit. If the answers of the text are at variance with my vision of life, or pre-understanding, I am forced to check my pre-understanding (at least to a degree and at least in part). In this way I can be corrected and changed by the text. Thus, in Bultmann's words, pre-understanding "does not have to be eliminated, but has to be raised to consciousness to be critically examined in the course of understanding a text, to be gambled with; in short, this is required: to allow oneself to be questioned during one's inquiry of the text and to listen to its claims."[24]

Normative exegesis takes place when we are keenly aware of our pre-understandings or visions rather than when we try to hide them. Then we are able to let the text speak in terms of the differences from and similarities with our own prejudices. Without such interaction interpreters easily, often unconsciously, trace their own visions and beliefs onto the text and then read them "objectively" out of the text. Ironic and paradoxical as it may seem, the more aware we are of the fore-beliefs and fore-conceptions of our own visions, the more we are able to do justice to the message of the text.

The importance of the hermeneutic circle, or, a term that seems more appropriate, the hermeneutic spiral (I imagine a spiral coil), is hard to overstate. It is in any case unavoidable, intrinsic to the human predicament. However, modern hermeneutic theory seems often to conceive of this spiral in overly psychologistic and subjectivistic terms.

In the tradition of Schleiermacher and Betti it is mandatory for interpretation that the interpreter live into the totality of an author's life and approximate the intellectual-spiritual stature of the author as closely as possible. This is to understand interpretation in terms of the "interpreter's own subjectivity attempting to grasp the subjectivity of the author's intentions or of the original addressee's reception of its meaning."[25]

However, that psychological approach stumbles on the reality that the inner life of an author, particularly of another culture, context, and time, always in the end remains hidden and irretrievable. Moreover, focus on the subjective inner experience of author or original readers ignores the fact that dialogue between persons takes place as an exchange between visions of life. Such dialogue is possible because worldviews of whatever time and of whatever origin share a common structure as responses to God's universal, constant and trans-temporal order which calls to life and makes for life. It is in terms of the dialogic confrontation of visions — competing answers to God's common, ultimate and abiding calls to life — rather than in an empathetic re-experiencing of the inner life or cultural situation of the author that the strangeness of another horizon may be overcome. It is in this kind of visionary exchange that we are able to understand (the vision of) a text. Then, as Gadamer would say, a fusion of horizons takes place: *Horizontverschmelzung.* Or, as I would add, a clash of horizons takes place. Understanding a text is not empathizing with the author, but understanding its basic vision or fundamental message.

Not only do many psychologize the hermeneutic spiral, but they get lost in it, as if that is all there is to reality. It is true that we experience reality in terms of a dialectic, spiral movement between self and world as macro-cosmic text. But the spiral neither contains nor constitutes all of reality. Reality is bigger than our experience of it. The spiral movement is the dynamic process in and by which we experience and respond to God's universal word for life and creation. Making the hermeneutic spiral all there is to reality can lead, and often does, to a side-stepping of the final question of whether or not the message or vision presented in the text is true or not.

The decisive question, said Heidegger, is not "to get out of the circle but to come into it in the right way."[26] That is indeed the important consideration. However, it is not that we have to follow a certain procedure to get into the circle properly: everyone enters the circle in the same way. It is not that one needs to enter the circle at the right place: any point in the circle is as good as any other for entry. If the discussion with which I began is on the right track, we enter the circle by accepting in terms of our traditions certain basic beliefs as truth (personally appropriated and articulated as the pre-understanding of a vision of life) in the surrender of faith. When everything is said and done, it is by revelation received in faith that we enter the circle.

The question then is not first of all, what are the proper procedures, but, how do we enter in truth with the right and proper revelation, i.e., a life-affirming revelation which offers freedom, dignity, hope and healing. For it is the received revelation which gives direction to our movement in the hermeneutic circle —

through articulation and conceptualization in a vision of life. The perceptions of a vision are the pre-understandings which guide our interpretation. When a text challenges our pre-understandings, we may have to rethink our own vision or worldview. At times, we may be so challenged that we give up our worldviews and the faith in which they are rooted. That is conversion and the acceptance of a new ultimate. In that case, we, so to speak, re-enter the circle in a new way, i.e., with new purpose, direction and ultimate meaning.

Hermeneutical spiral and scriptural interpretation

Interpretation as the dialogic spiral between an interpreter's vision and the text's vision is of great importance for biblical interpretation. For it is not Jeremiah's view, Paul's opinions or the situations of Ruth and Rahab that we share. Nor is it necessary that we do, any more than we need to share David's feelings and Mary's emotions. But we can — and ought to — share their integrating vision, their overarching perspective, their faith certitudes.

Focusing on a specific text of Scripture will further illustrate the realities as well as the complexities of the hermeneutic spiral. Christians, looking for instruction in daily living, may turn to the Sermon on the Mount in Matthew 5:38-42.

> *Do not resist one who is evil. But if any one strikes you on the right cheek, turn to him the other also; and if any one would sue you and take your coat, let him have your cloak as well; and if any one forces you to go one mile, go with him two miles. Give to him who begs from you, and do not refuse him who would borrow from you.*

The answer of the text to the initial queries for guidance gives rise to various responses. "Isn't that a rather high price to pay for following Christ?" "Impossible!" "Nonsensical, out-of-this-world idealism!" "I must be a bad Christian because I can't do that!" The initial responses lead to re-readings of the text with revised expectations and questions. Does the context modify the demands? What is the context? Who is Jesus really talking to? Are we to take his words literally? Can anyone really be a Christian in this world? And on and on.

A back and forth dialogue between the text and the interpreter ensues. Gradually the differences between the vision of the interpreter and that of the text are worked through. The process comes to (at least temporary) conclusion through a fusing of visions or horizons. Or a more fundamental clashing. Some conclude that full Christian service means always turning the other cheek and giving away possessions to anyone who asks. Some of these readers, despite the difficulty, try to life accordingly; others find themselves unable to obey and develop tremendous guilt complexes; others may turn their backs on the Gospel because of its impossible demands. Another group of readers judge that Jesus is setting forth the ideal Christian ethic which holds only for the church and which need not and cannot be realized in the rest of the life or in this dispensation. Others take solace in the belief that Jesus is only speaking metaphorically (*The New Jerusalem Bible*, readers edition, appends a note that verse 40 is "deliberately hyperbolic"). Yet another group concludes that Jesus is listing the *kind* of radical actions that are demanded of those who wholeheartedly seek first the kingdom of heaven and God's righteousness (Matt. 6:33), leaving it up to our responsibility in the Spirit to do similar kinds of things today.

On a broader front, the same hermeneutic complexity is illustrated by the continuing controversy in New Testament scholarship about the political content of Jesus' life and preaching. Recently Rosemary Ruether has argued that thinkers (such as S. G. E. Brandon) who see Jesus as basically a nationalist, political revolutionary as well as scholars (such as Martin Hengel and Oscar Cullmann) who see Jesus' messianism as basically eschatological and personal, having nothing to do with the actual socio-political unrest, skew the biblical message. Having adopted "the basic Greek dualism between the inward and the outward, the spiritual and the social, time and eternity" as their vision, they see Jesus in terms of this dualism. Brandon "reduces messianism to secular politics and Hengel and Cullmann spiritualize it."[27] If we reject such as dualistic vision as Greek and consider a "holistic," both-and vision to be eminently biblical, Ruether suggests that we will also recognize that the Jesus portrayed in Scripture was a prophet whose message calls for a spiritual-political liberation in this world, liberation from all systems of domination. These examples illustrate that not only is exegesis a hermeneutic spiral between the vision of the interpreter and the vision implied in the text, but also that basic exegetical disagreements are more a result of competing worldviews than a matter of textual detail.[28]

Sense, reference, and decision

5. Interpretation is a three-level act of whole persons, guided

by their visions (or pre-understandings) of life, deeply affected
by their emotional state and their socio-economic situation.

There are, it seems to me, three reciprocally relating levels in
any act of interpretation. I will refer to them as the "semantic"
level, the "meaning" level, and the "decisional" level.[29] In one
direction, attention to semantic symbols is foundational to the
determination of meaning and, likewise, discernment of meaning is
prior to any decision in response to that meaning. At the same
time, in an opposite direction, we come to the text and are guided
in our reading of the text by our pre-understandings (as decisions
previously made). Such pre-understandings help us locate the
meaning-world of the text which we in turn relate to the semantic
symbols of the text. The simultaneous interaction of these two di-
rections — what could be called the "foundational" direction from
semantic to decisional, and the "transcendental" direction from
decisional to semantic — witnesses to the fact that a hermeneutic
spiral takes place not only between interpreter and text but also
within the three levels of the interpretive act itself.

Analogous to the foundational, lingual nature of a text, interpretation is a lingually founded activity (level one). Without
attention to symbols, interpretation does not take place, just as
without symbols there is no text. Level one is the explanation of
the immanent lingual sense of the semantic text. What are the
possible meanings of the text? This level seems to receive the
emphasis in much of analytic philosophy and in schools of
linguistics, including structuralism.

But a purely semantic elucidation remains suspended until the
symbols are related to their world of reference, the subject-matter
of the text. Level two is interpreting the lingual symbols in reference to what they refer to extra-lingually. Depending on the particular mode of being in the world which the interpreter adopts to
decipher the extra-lingual reference, interpretive acts become
typical acts of, for example, political, economic, aesthetic, moral,
faith, or philosophical interpretation. It is when interpreters
assume the *same* mode of relation to the text that is incorporated
in the text that proper interpretation can take place. In other
words, understanding a text depends on sharing the same sphere of
meaning as that text. Thus, an economic text asks first of all to be
interpreted economically, a political text politically, and a
certitudinal (faith) text from the faith perspective of certitude.
When the reader's way of relating to the text does not appro-
priately match the prevailing perspective incorporated in the

text, the text is violated and interpretation will be significantly distorted.

While level one attends to the lingual symbols in the light of and guided by the interpreter's perception of a certain kind of extra-lingual referent, level two attends to the world of extra-lingual meaning in light of and guided by the lingual symbols. While level one begins with individual words, sentences, and paragraphs, construing the whole in terms of the details, level two begins with an intuitive grasping of the text as a whole, recognizing the details in terms of the whole. Interpretation is the dialogic process of testing and validating the intuitive grasping of the whole — what Ricoeur following Hirsch calls "a guess"[30] — in terms of the parts. Semantical investigation of what is said is foundational to determining what the text is about. At the same time, description of linguistic forms is in important respects affected by prior understanding of what the text is about.

To understand a text the interpreter must apprehend and acknowledge the meaning-intentions embodied in the verbal expressions. These intentions always hold together and are shaped in terms of one of the fundamental ways of being in the world. They belong together, cohere and make sense in terms of one of these modes of being and its particular realm of discourse, form of life, sphere of meaning or "language-game." Sensitivity to the text's underlying and pervasive sphere of meaning allows readers to tune in to the wave length of the text. Tuning in to *that* particular angle of approach incorporated in the text, interpreters are enabled to sort out the fundamental meaning of the text in terms of *that* mode of being.

Although, as I have just noted, honoring the integrity of a specific text calls for recognition of and attunement to the dominant mode or angle of vision presented in that text, it would be wrong to conclude that it is illegitimate to interpret a text from vantage points afforded by modes of reality other than the mode in which the text presents itself. But such interpretive endeavors need to be continually mindful of the text's dominant or qualifying focus. For example, an economic interpretation of Scripture must acknowledge openly that economic matters in the Scriptures are not addressed economically, i.e., from the economic angle of vision, but always from the certitudinal-faith angle. The economic teaching of the Scripture is embedded in discourse which bears a certitudinal focus and purpose. Consequently, for example, the various economic policies described in Scripture, whether the

Mosaic regulations concerning property, tithing or interest or the all-things-in-common practice of the New Testament church in Acts 2, cannot properly be called the straightforward message of Scripture, as if the Scriptures were a textbook in economics. What the Scriptures do proclaim in and through their faith treatment of economic realities is that God is the Supreme Owner of all that is and that we are caretakers of creation, called to a stewardship of creation's resources in loving service to neighbor and God. Not explicit economic rules, but the abiding norms of stewardship, caring for and sharing with the poor and needy are the biblical message. How in our day and age we are to work out these abiding norms in concrete economic measures is our challenge and responsibility. Thus, a proper economic interpretation of Scriptures is a certitudinal-economic interpretation in which the Scripture via its certitudinal focus fundamentally calls us to the norm of stewardship in the area of economic life. That is, the Bible gives *general* guidance and direction in a way that demands the hearer's *specific* response.

Level three: dialogue and decision
This demand for response brings us to the third level of the interpretive act. Level three is the on-going dialogue in which, guided by their own vision of life, interpreters engage the message of the text. Here interpretation demands that readers open themselves up to the text and face the claims of the text and its meaning for their own lives. It means allowing the pre-conceptions and pre-understandings of our own visions to be critically tested and reviewed. Interpretation on this level is the on-going process of risking our own world-vision in encounter with the world disclosed in the text. It means being personally open to change, clarification, cleansing, and renewal. It means decision. Either we allow ourselves to be corrected by the text and take appropriate action, or we are confirmed in our positions and leave, strengthened in conviction.

The kinds of decisions, their significance and scope, will be largely set by the kinds of meaning-intentions which emerge in level two. An appropriate response to a theoretic argument will be of the kind: let me think about it. How-to books on health care, auto repair, home renovations, or playing the stock markets serve their guiding purpose when readers develop new capacities or sharpen old abilities. Apt responses to a good story may range widely, but begin with: "that's a great story!" or "that reminds me of a story." Texts which offer insight into ourselves, our institutions and our relations ask that in response we deepen our insight and change our actions. However, whatever the kind of text, whatever the appropriate kind of response, or regardless of the way the material is presented, indirectly and implicitly a dialogue between worldviews is taking place. Such worldview to-the-roots dialogue often becomes explicit and direct when, for whatever reasons and whatever the topic, the interpreter feels out of synch with the text. When the ultimate claims which are implicit in the text confront the ultimate beliefs of the interpreter, a fundamental sorting out becomes necessary.

The implicit or indirect dialogue between worldviews which is an important reality in all interpretation is explicit and direct in the interpretation of certitudinal texts. An appropriate response to a certitudinal text is of the order of: Yes, I receive that as the Truth, and commit myself to live by it, or, No, I reject that as False, and commit myself to fight against it. The fact that a Yes/No decision with far-reaching ramifications is the relevant kind of response to such texts makes clear that their inter-pretation has an unusual feature. In reading certitudinal texts the "decisional" level not only plays its leading role implicitly or as a third subsequent phase or level, but the decisional is virtually coalesced with the second "meaning" level of interpretation. Especially in reading certitudinal texts, the dialogue, risk and encounter between worldviews which characterizes level three is already directly involved in level two interpretation. That is why, as we have noted earlier, an open receptivity to the pervasive message of the text promotes proper interpretation and a closed heart obstructs proper interpretation.

All three levels — the semantic, meaning and decisional — are reciprocally operative in any interpretive act. And usually the focus at any one time is more on one level than on the others. Failure to give each level or phase its due results in unfinished or inadequate interpretation. While explanation of the semantic sense of the text is foundational to interpretation, it has become increasingly clear that interpreters are guided throughout the process by their pre-understandings or visions of life.

Emotional anxiety and societal privilege

The importance of pre-understanding has, since Bultmann, been recognized. What has not been sufficiently taken into conside-ration, however, is that a vision of life is not as pure or as trans-parent to its adherents as they often assume. Ricoeur judges that modern hermeneutics is still too smug and self-assured about the transparency of the self-consciousness. "Marx, Nietzsche, and Freud," he says, "have taught us to unmask its tricks."[31]

The point is that a vision of life is not the pure product of faith. Often our emotional anxieties and hidden desires to maintain our socio-economic positions of power lead us to adopt beliefs which legitimatize and justify these motivations rather than face and deal with them. We rationalize and construct ideologies ("not being transparent-to-oneself...is the defining characteristic of "ideology").[32] In short, we are often induced to adopt a vision of life which hides us from ourselves by putting a good face on a bad thing.

It is the critical hermeneutics[33] of Habermas and the Frankfurt school along with Paul Ricoeur that has been particularly perceptive at just this point. Gadamer, they say, is still idealist in his inability and unwillingness to consider the extra-linguistic factors such as economic-material conditions and other unconscious motivations which lead to distorted communication, domination, half-lies, propaganda and repression.

We need to take more seriously that our Christian visions of life can also be clouded by emotional anxieties and the illusions they nourish. In this context such seriousness is crucial because distorted visions lead us to locate in the Scriptures what, in fact, are our own emotionally rooted illlusions and fears. If, for example, racist, sexist, oppressive, escape-this-world, body-is-evil kind of beliefs become part of our vision, we will find justification for them in Scripture.

If healing breakthroughs are going to take place in the Christian church on these issues, more exegesis of relevant texts is not enough. We need exegesis which more forthrightly compares and confronts the basic visions involved; only in this way can hidden motivations be unearthed and addressed. Change in interpretation on basic matters does happen. Usually, it occurs as the consequences of changes in one's personal-societal life. Life experiences begin to lead to questions about previous ways of seeing reality. Out of the ensuing crisis comes a modified vision of life with its possibilities for revised exegesis.

Vision of text and authorial intention

    6. The message, thrust, vision or subject-matter of the text,
    and not authorial intention, is essential to proper inter-
    pretation.

Some interpreters (Betti, Hirsch and, I judge, the majority of evangelical interpreters[34]) stress the need to determine the objective meaning of a text through methodological efforts to make precise the original author's intention. Redaction criticism is one such method. Schleiermacher and Betti have emphasized the need to re-experience, re-think and re-construct what the author had originally thought and felt. Others set out to determine the original situation or *Sitz im Leben* which called forth the original text. More recently, others tend toward socio-cultural analyses of the communities which were the first historical addressees of the text.

No doubt all these ways can be most helpful and can easily be recommended. Information about all these background matters helps, sometimes dramatically, in interpretation. But to hinge the validity of interpretation on whether or not the author's intention or original situation is captured is, I believe, a serious mistake. To emphasize that the meaning of a text can be determined by "divination" (Dilthey: *Einfühlung*) of the author's intention in an empathetic and imaginative re-enactment of the inner life of the author seems to me highly psychologistic. Of course, there is an intimate connection between the meaning of a text and authorial intention. The text owes its origin to the author. It is situated in a certain context. But after the text is written, the text is distanced from its author and from its original situation. These are, as Ricoeur puts it, "behind" the text. But they are not the text itself. A text has its own life. In written discourse authorial intention and the meaning of the text do not always continue to coincide. In terms of Scripture, sometimes the canonical context invites a reading which is even against the original intent of an author or makes such an intent irrelevant to the claim of Scripture. A written text escapes, in important ways, the very limited horizon of its author.[35]

Ricoeur concludes that one need not know the authorial intention in order to understand the text. I think he is right. *What* the text says matters now much more than what the author meant to say. In fact, the author may have mis-spoken him/ herself. It is a well-known phenomenon that authors are often blind themselves to conceptual shifts or changes that have occurred in their written texts. Moreover, how can one ever re-experience or re-think the inner life of another person? Gadamer seems on target when he judges that if there is anything to such re-enactment of inner meaning, it is in imagining oneself to be in the *what* the author's thoughts are about, rather than to be in the thoughts of the author him/herself.

Not only is inversion of the creation process a most hazardous undertaking, but historical-critical analysis, for all its value, has often left us with a dismantled text and no agreed-upon meaning. All these ways can contribute to interpretation, but, in my judgment, the aim of interpretation must center on the subject matter, the *what is said*, of the text. The text must be primarily understood from within itself. The aim is not the so-called objective reproduction of authorial meaning behind the text, but the delineation of the message or vision which is fixed in the text, "in front of" the text as Ricoeur expresses it.[36] I like the way David Tracy puts it: "The author of interest for the interpreter of the text's meanings is not the author as reconstructed, for example, by psycho-historical methods. Rather the particular vision of the author on reality becomes the self-referent of the text itself."[37] One can talk of an implied "author," "that personal vision of the world codified in or referred to by the oeuvre of any particular author." What I am saying is that texts have their own meaning which is no longer adequately described in terms of the author's original intention. The authorial intention and extra-textual determinants are important. How they are important remains a crucial question for continuing investigation. But they cannot be the main focus of interpretation. Nor are they the key to interpretation. The key is the message, vision, or as Ricoeur calls it, the "world" of the text. It is that "world," that message, which is up front and which needs to shine through if there is to be understanding of the text.

The fact that a written text may escape the limited horizon of author and first readers is of supreme importance: it makes interpretation of a text from another time and culture possible. In distinction from spoken words, a written text has a semantic autonomy from its context of origin which, in principle, makes conversation possible across the centuries. Reading is the "'remedy' by which the meaning of the text is 'rescued' from the estrangement and distantiation and put in a new proximity."[38] When we further realize that the main key to interpreting a text is the "what" of the text rather than its inimitable and irretrievable "when," "where," or "how," the possibility of overcoming the distance through an appropriation of the "what" presented in the text is even more promising. That, of course, does not make interpretation easy: the "what" always comes cloaked with a where, when and how. But it does make interpretation possible. And even though we are always struggling against distantiation, the estrangement can be overcome in a fusion of horizons which is the meeting of "worlds."

Centering attention on the message or "world" codified in the text is also of crucial importance because it makes clear that the decisional or existential moment of interpretation (how do I respond to the text?) follows upon an interpretation of the message of the text.

A Heideggerian-Bultmannian hermeneutic tends to focus so exclusively on this existential moment that the meaning of the text is reduced to its meaning for me. The text is treated as a jumping-off place from which one can go anywhere. What is crucial, then, is the decision, the event of revelation, e.g. Fuchs' *Sprachereignis* or Ebeling's *Wortgeschehen*,[39] which transforms my life. In the process the normative question of understanding the message of the text correctly is shunted aside as being of secondary consequence. The critical point here is not that the decisional moment is unimportant. Without it, as we have observed, interpretation remains unfinished. But when the decisional moment, rather than the text, becomes the meaning to be interpreted, the hermeneutic enterprise goes awry.

Scripture interpreting scripture

In deciphering the message of the text, we need to search for an interpretation which makes the text maximally coherent and maximally consistent with itself. Gadamer talks of a "prejudice of perfection"[40] in this context. We assume the unity or perfection of a text when we first approach it. To do otherwise is to preclude genuine understanding of the text before one has ever begun. The whole is to be understood in light of its parts, and the parts in light of the whole. A provisional interpretation of parts needs to be checked against global interpretation, and a provisional idea of the global which emerges in reading the parts must also be checked against the parts.

This is, of course, a hermeneutic circle of which exegetes of Scripture have long been aware. The Reformers talked of the Analogy of Scripture: Scripture should be interpreted by Scripture; the secondary and obscure needs to be interpreted in light of the primary and plain. Text and context are to be interpreted in dialectic interrelation. That, incidentally, by no means implies inattention to extra-textual materials. Such investigation is required, but for the purpose of arriving at a global understanding of the vision of the text which fits internally with all the givens of the text.

A clearer focus in biblical studies on the elucidation of the "vision" of the text of Scripture rather than on authorial intention and original *Sitz im Leben* would, I believe, be fruitful. Many of the authors of Scriptures are anonymous, a redactor's intent may differ from that of the original author, a book may have multiple authors from different times. All that is in the end secondary to the vision or central thrust of the text.

Moreover, understanding the original situation of the text does not mean we have interpreted the text, if what needs understanding is the message of the text. Since this vision is fleshed out in a text written in a specific time, by specific authors, historical-critical investigations are invaluable. But their focus must be on illuminating the message of the text as given rather than on determining the authenticity and historicity of the text.

For when all is said and done, it is the content of the message of the Scripture that is crucial. In my view the critical challenge is to investigate how all the individual pericopes, sections, books, and testaments, in their diversity and plurality, contribute to, expand, enrich, and embroider the single, central unified message of the Scriptures: new life in Christ for the whole cosmos.

Dwelling in this pre-understanding of the central thrust of Scripture, interpreters can trace the certitudinal thrust of a particular text in terms of its immediate context, in terms of a specific book, and finally in terms of the place of the book in the canon as a whole. In and through attending to details of time, place and purpose, the particular text's abiding certitudinal message of exhortation, hope, judgment, promise, and surety becomes clearer. This reading is enriched by widening our horizons to the context of the whole book: each book arose in specific circumstances and was written to serve a specific certitudinal purpose. Since a specific certitudinal purpose guided the writers in their selection and arrangement of materials, awareness of that purpose can enhance our understanding of the nuances which a common biblical theme may exhibit in a particular text. Reading an entire biblical book in one sitting often helps to deepen our sense of its dominant motifs. And constructing an outline of a book with focus on the development of these key motifs can further enrich our sense both of the global meaning of the book and of the fit of the parts. When the Evangelists, for example, present differing sequences of events, the question is not: Who made the error? but, What certitudinal purpose was served by arranging the material in that way? Attending to the particular demands which their writings were addressing, Richard Longenecker, to take a telling example, has demonstrated that the different emphases of Paul, James and Hebrews on "faith" need not be read as tensions or contradictions which either require us to harmonize or take sides.[41]

Such comparing of diverse scriptural portrayals of themes or events, tracing cross-references, and highlighting key words is further enhanced by attention to the architectonic place of each book in the canonic whole. The Pentateuchal "*Torah* of the priest" (see Jeremiah 18:18 and Matthew 23:34) formed the foundation and touchstone of the Old Testament covenantal community. The *Torah* was God's gift of guidance so that life had shape, purpose and perspective. The *Torah* is followed by the "word of the prophet," early and later, major and minor commentaries on the fractured life of the community, surprising new words of God in continuity with the *Torah*, calling to repentance, witnessing to deliverance and God'sfaithfulness. And the prophetic books are interspersed by the "counsel of the wise," writings, rooted in the *Torah*, praising God who makes and saves us, and instructing us about the way to knowledge through engagement with the world as created order.[42] In the New Testament the Gospels are the Good News of redemption and recreation in Jesus Christ which, fulfilling the *Torah* (cf. Luke 10:26), the writings, and the prophets and writings relate to the *Torah*, Acts, Revelation and the letters are books of exhortation (cf. Hebrews 13:22), instructing, warning, and encouraging the New Testament Church, proclaiming and witnessing to the growth of the Kingdom of God that is already here and is still coming.

The exegetical process is a spiral "round and round" move-ment between a global or canonic understanding of the meaning of a text which guides attention to the particular text, and attention to the details and immediate context of the text as a test of the global meaning. In the on-going conversation the particular vision or message of the text becomes clearer.

Certitudinal history
History in the Scriptures is certitudinally qualified history. It is no more or less historical than economic, political, or general cultural histories. But just as these kinds of histories have their own distinct focus, as do histories of music and art, sport and recreation, certitudinal history is written with a distinct focus: ultimate realities, ultimate questions and ultimate certainty.

Luke sets out to write a history of "all that Jesus began both to do and to teach" (Acts 1:1).[43] The book of Joshua is not just a collection of isolated stories from the history of Israel. Nor is it a biography of Joshua or a politico-military account of the conquest of Canaan. "It is the story of how Yahweh fulfilled His promise to give Israel possession of the land of rest. The whole book is carefuly constructed so that each episode develops this central theme."[44]

The writer of Kings, much to the chagrin of some modern critics, says very little about Solomon's extensive building program; rather, he chooses to deal with the building of just the temple — in profuse detail. Omri, who by all cultural accounts was a far more significant king than his son Ahab, is given but a few verses. Ahab, by contrast, is described in a flourish of detail because in his reign the people of Israel hit a new low in disobedience to Yahweh. While little information is given about Hezekiah's extensive reforms, a half chapter is devoted to the healing of a boil on Hezekiah's body because it was "a sign that Yahweh recognized Hezekiah's obedience."[45]

The book of Kings is not a collection of royal biographies, nor a general, cultural history but a history focused on explaining to a people in exile that their sorry plight is the result of human disobedience. The people of Israel led by their Kings, not Yahweh, had failed to keep the covenant. When we are guided by that focus on obedience/disobedience to Yahweh — what I refer to structurally as the certitudinal focus — we are in possession of a key which helps us better understand the selection and presentation of materials. We also acquire a good start in understanding the discrepancies between Kings and Chronicles. In contrast to the concern of Samuel-Kings to show that the exile was punishment for breaking the Covenant, the Chronicler is concerned to encourage the post-exilic community to new acts of obedience. Sin, he wants to make clear, always brings judgment, while obedience yields peace and justice. To that purpose he makes David and Solomon nearly faultless and reshapes the accounts of the reigns of many of the individual kings.[46]

Talk of certitudinal history offers us, I suggest, a fundamental re-orientation away from and beyond the history/story, reality/myth debate which polarizes much of biblical studies.[47]

Biblical narratives are neither myth nor general, cultural history, but historical stories both written from and for a specialized certitudinal purpose of engendering and exhorting faith. Only when we do justice to the specialized purpose of the canonic texts are we able to honor them in their received form even as we engage in critical interpretation.

Certitudinal exegesis: a hermeneutics of ultimacy
The crucial role that the certitudinal dynamics occupy in regard to
Scriptural exegesis leads me to question whether either the historico-critical methods of the higher critics or the traditional grammatical-historical method is adequate. Neither method, I would
judge, has sufficiently in purview the distinctive structural focus
which gives contours to biblical revelation. I am suggesting that
we would do well to talk of certitudinal exegesis,[48] an exegesis
which, true to its object of investigation, is pastoral in intention
and is illumined by historical criticism and grammatical-
linguistic studies. The development of a hermeneutics of ultimacy
would, among other things, cause us to take more seriously the fact
that the focus of Scripture is neither primarily grammatical, historical, nor literary. A focus on the dynamics of certitude would
also make clear that psychologistic, economistic, moralistic or
intellectualistic readings of Scripture are inappropriate.

That does not mean that psychological or socio-economic
insights offer no help in reading the Bible. Indeed, psychology, in
particular Jungian psychology with its attention to the subcon-
scious dynamics of our inner life, can help us nourish an inner
capacity which heightens our sensitivity to the biblical message.
Socio-economic theories can alert us not only to the impact of
changing socio-economic conditions on biblical revelation, but also
to the role socio-economic location plays in our own biblical interpretation. Nor does a hermeneutics of certitude deny that the
Bible is literature, has cognitive content and that it speaks to our
moral life. The point is that reading the Scripture as literature,
with its cognitive content and with its concern for the moral life
without due and proper attention to its governing focus on the
certitude of faith is to ask Scripture to be what it is not. Scripture
is not a moral handbook, a systematic treatise, a collection of
psychotherapeutic case-histories, a literary anthology, or a series of socio-political histories.

Emphasis on the certitudinal would also make clear that the
cognitive content of Scripture is certitudinally qualified. Scripture is not a theoretic text filled with analytically qualified
theoretic propositions. The lingual discourse of Scripture does
have cognitive content, but the cognitive content is taken up, subsumed, and presented in terms of a certitudinal-faith focus on the
ultimates. In contrast to the abstract, universalizing, structure-
describing character of theoretic (including theological) discourse,
certitudinal discourse has a cumulative, telescopic, perspectival,
no if's or but's, encountering quality. In other words, Scriptural

truths are to be read and understood as visionary, ultimate, certitudinal truths. The contrast in the Scriptures is between truth (as faithfulness) and lying (as instability, swerving from the truth) rather than between truth (as scientific precision) and errancy (as limited or defective information). God promises in the Spirit of Christ (John 14:26) to be covenantally faithful and invites us to listen to God's voice in the Scriptures. We can count on the Scriptures, for they record the Word of the faithful one. They will never lead us astray in connection with the ultimate questions of life. On that depth-level they are true and inerrant.

Our exegetical task is greatly enhanced when we realize that attention to the certitudinal focus enables us to zero in on the abiding message of a text given to us in all its time-conditionedness. What a biblical text proclaims, informs, celebrates, narrates, etc., about the basic questions of life, the ultimates, is abiding.

We are in fact delivered from a kind of biblicism which seeks a specific proof-text in order to live out the Gospel message in all the various areas of life. The biblical answers to the ultimate questions of life direct and guide us as we give concrete form to our lives by attending to the creational dynamics of the various areas of life. In this way, that is, via their focus on the ultimates of life, the Scriptures exercise total and full authority with a range as wide as creation. Envisioning from Scripture what God wants for our lives, we are empowered in the Spirit of God to re-envision that life-giving message in relevant specifics that make for healing and hope in our troubled times.

Since the Scriptures make known to us that it is by the Word of God that the heavens and earth were made (Heb. 11:3), that it is by the "same Word" that they are still sustained (II Peter 3:7), and that it is the same Word that was made flesh for our redemption (John 1:1,18), we know that in the Spirit of Christ we can move surely and freely in God's creation (II Cor. 5:17; Gal. 5:1). Revealing the possibility of new life in Jesus Christ, the Scriptures invite us to change our ways and participate anew as co-partners with God in caring for creation by responding to and unfolding the meaning of justice, mercy, stewardship, health, clarity, fidelity, consistency — all of God's creative Words of Love — for creation and all its creatures. Knowing and trusting that God's Word of Love holds dynamically for all of life, we are empowered in the Spirit to search out and apply it relevantly and creatively to life in our times in all its facets.

Because of the Fall into sin, we need the Spirit of God to

renew us and the "glasses" of Scripture to teach us how, in love and by grace, to discern what God intended from the beginning. The Bible is one, single, long, true story of the Covenantal Rule of God — which has come and which is acoming — claiming humanity and all of creation, promising shalom in Jesus Christ through the Spirit. We are named and commissioned, sustained and grounded in our identity and integrity as servant-heirs of God. We learn who we are, where we are, what we need, where we are headed, and what our calling is.

The Scriptures are the story of redemption: the Word of God inscripturated in human words for our healing and instruction. Translated into terminology germane to this essay, the Scriptures are a redemptive rearticulation/republication of the Word of God in certitudinal-lingual focus. Since the Bible speaks redemptively in human words what God said from the beginning and continues to say, the Bible's central message is immediately relevant to all of life in all times and places. It is when we honor the certitudinal focus in which the message comes and ask questions accordingly that we are able to experience its direct relevance. Then we are aided and abetted in using and experiencing the BIble as the Bible itself promises — as profitable for teaching, exhorting, comfort and encouragement.[50]

In the last three paragraphs, I have sketched my own understanding of a biblical vision of life and briefly related it to our previous discussion. I have included it to give readers a more concrete idea of the vision which orients and guides me in interpreting the text of Scripture. I have not presented and do not intend to present a case for this particular understanding.[51] What I have done — at least intended to do — is to argue the crucial importance of both the interpreter's vision and the vision of the text in interpretation.

Call to discussion
If my treatment of the hermeneutic dynamics is at all on target, we are called to renewed comparison and discussion of our various life perspectives or visions of life which are the glasses which frame and color what we read. An important part of such discussions will be the comparing of our various proposals about the nature of Scripture as a whole. For unless we seriously discuss the nature of the scriptural text, the kinds of questions which are appropriate and inappropriate to it and the appropriate perspective from which to ask our questions, we will continue to exegete particular texts of Scripture not only with differences of

emphasis — necessary and understandable — but in very diverse, contrasting and even contradictory ways. In order to make more credible our unity as the Body of Christ and to take steps toward healing, new understanding and rapprochement, such wide-ranging, cordial and open-hearted conversations are essential. Moreover, despite differences in articulated perspectives, as our common allegiance to the God of the Scriptures in the Spirit of Christ becomes a felt experience, our motivation will increase to reach out in unified efforts of witness and action towards healing, peace, and justice in our troubled world.

NOTES

1. James Packer, "Hermeneutics and Biblical Authority," *Themelios*, 5 (1975), p. 3. Cf. also D. A. Carson, "Hermeneutics: A Brief Assessment of Some Recent Trends," *Themelios*, 5 (1980), pp. 12-20.
2. Paul Ricoeur, *Freud and Philosophy* (New Haven: Yale University Press, 1970), p. 20-56.
3. Michael Polanyi, *The Tacit Dimension* (Garden City, N.Y.: Doubleday, 1966). John V. Apczynski has explored these matters extensively in his analysis of human cognitional activity based on the epistemology of Michael Polanyi. Cf. his *Doers of the Word* (Missoula, Montana: Scholars Press, 1977), esp. ch. 5, pp. 155-180. For an ideal of religious knowledge based on Polanyi, see Jerry H. Gill, *The Possibility of Religious Knowledge* (Grand Rapids: Eerdmans, 1971).
4. Langdon Gilkey, *Naming the Whirlwind* (Indianapolis: Bobbs-Merrill, 1969), pp. 426-427.
5. Ludwig Wittgenstein, *Philosophical Investigations*, Section 217 (Oxford: Blackwells, 1967).
6. Ludwig Wittgenstein, *On Certainty*, 88, 210, 211, 343 (New York: Harper Torchbooks, 1969), pp. 13e, 29e, 44e.
7. Cf. Hendrik Hart, "The Articulation of Belief: A Link between Rationality and Commitment," in *Rationality and the Calvinian Tradition*, eds. H. Hart, J. van der Hoeven & N. Wolterstorff (Lanham: University Press of America, 1983); Michael Polanyi, *Personal Knowledge* (London: Routledge and Kegan Paul, 1958); and Morris Kline, *The Loss of Certainty* (Oxford: Oxford University Press, 1980).
8. Kline, *op. cit.*, p. 316.
9. John Hick, *Faith and Knowledge* (Ithaca: Cornell University Press, 1957), p. 129.

10. John Calvin, *Institutes of the Christian Religion*, I.VII, 5 (Philadelphia: The Westminster Press, 1960), p. 80.

11. Gilkey, *op. cit.*, pp. 441-444. Cf. also A. Whitehead, *Modes of Thought* (New York: Macmillan, 1938). "Upon the presupposition of the evidence, all understanding rests....It follows that philosophy in any proper sense of the term, cannot be proved," p. 67.

12. David H. Kelsey, *The Uses of Scripture in Recent Theology* (Philadelphia: Fortress Press, 1975), esp. chaps. 8 and 9. Also the review by Carl F. H. Henry, "Theology and Biblical Authority: A Review Article," in *Journal of the Evangelical Theological Society*, 19 (Fall, 1976), pp. 315-323.

13. Cf. Gerhard Ebeling, *Word and Faith* (London: SCM, 1963), p. 318 in H.-G. Gadamer, *Truth and Method* (London: Sheed and Ward, 1975), p. 350.

14. Cf. E. D. Hirsch, "Current Issues in Theory of Interpretation," in *Journal of Religion*, July, 1974, p. 303.

15. Paul Ricoeur, *Interpretation Theory: Discourse and the Surplus of Meaning* (Fort Worth: Texas Christian University Press, 1976), p. 76.

16. Cf. Josef Bleicher, *Contemporary Hermeneutics* (Boston: Routledge & Kegan Paul, 1980), p. 224. Anthony Thiselton takes note of the diverse ways structuralists tend to go in the final step of interpretation in *The Two Horizons* (Grand Rapids: Eerdmans, 1980), p. 429. For an introduction to structuralism, see Daniel Patte, *What is Structural Analysis?* (Philadelphia: Fortress Press, 1976) and Robert Detweiler, *Story, Sign, and Self* (Philadelphia: Fortress Press, 1978).

17. David Tracy, *Blessed Rage for Order* (New York: Seabury Press, 1975), p. 55.

18. Cf. my "On Worldviews," *Christian Scholar's Review* 14/2 (1985), pp. 153-164 for elaboration of the certitudinal way of being in the world as well as the nature and function of a vision of life. For an earlier attempt to articulate a hermeneutics of certitude, see my "Towards a Certitudinal Hermeneutic" in *Hearing and Doing*, ed. John Kraay and Anthony Tol (Toronto: Wedge Publishing Foundation, 1979).

19. My concern to help recover a new sense of the unity of Scripture while attendant to its diversity is very similar to Brevard Childs' admirable efforts to search for a new consensus by viewing the Bible as canon. See Brevard S. Childs, *Introduction to the Old Testament as Scripture* (Philadelphia: Fortress Press, 1979). *The New Testament as Canon: An Introduction* (Phila-

delphia: Fortress Press, 1984) and Gerald T. Sheppard, "Canonization: Hearing the Voice of the Same God in Historically Dissimilar Traditions," *Interpretation* 36/1 (1982), pp. 21-33.

20. One of the best introductions to modern hermeneutics is still James M. Robinson's essay, "Hermeneutic Since Barth," in *The New Hermeneutic* (Philadelphia: Fortress, 1964), eds. James Robinson and John B. Cobb. Anthony Thiselton's *The Two Horizons* knowledgeably and clearly discusses biblical exegetical concerns with special reference to Heidegger, Bultmann, Gadamer and Wittgenstein. Cf. also Carl Braaten, *History and Hermeneutics* (Philadelphia: Westminster, 1966), Richard E. Palmer, *Hermeneutics* (Evanston: Northwestern University Press, 1969), Robert W. Funk, *Language, Hermeneutic, and the Word of God* (New York: Harper & Row, 1966), Paul Achtemeier, *An Introduction to the New Hermeneutic* (Philadelphia:Westminster, 1969) and Walter Wink, *The Bible in Human Transformation: Towards a New Paradigm for Biblical Study* (Philadelphia: Fortress, 1973).

21. Heidegger talked of the *Vorhabe, Vorsicht* and *Vorgriff* which make up what Bultmann called *Vorverständnis.* Cf. Heidegger, *Being and Time* #32 (New York: Harper and Row, 1962), pp. 188-195 and Bultmann, *Essays: Philosophical and Theological* (London: SCM Press, 1950), p. 239.

22. Emilio Betti has become known through his two volume *Terio Generale della Interpretazione* (Milan: Dott. A Giuffre, ed. Instituto di Teoria della Interpretazione, 1955) in which he revitalizes such an objective-idealist approach to hermeneutics in contrast especially to Gadamer. In 1962 he summarized his work in one essay "Die Hermeneutik als allgemeine Methode der Geisterswissenschaften." Bleicher has translated this essay and includes it in his volume, pp. 51-94. E. D. Hirsch, Jr. is the leading American adherent of Betti's approach. Cf. his *Validity in Interpretation* (New Haven: Yale University Press, 1967) and *The Aims of Interpretation* (Chicago: University of Chicago Press, 1976).

23. Especially Gadamer and Paul Ricoeur have been very critical of the Cartesian model. "It is with *Freud and Philosophy* that I broke away from the illusions of consciousness as the blind spot of reflection," P. Ricoeur in "Toward a Hermeneutic of the Idea of Revelation," *The Harvard Theological Review*, Vol. 70 (1977), p. 28. Cf. Bleicher, pp. 248-251. It is in the work and writings of Paul Ricoeur that modern hermeneutical conflicts are mediated and at least to some extent overcome. He attempts to do

justice to the integrity of the text without minimizing the significant role of pre-conceptions or the impact of extra-linguistic matters both personal and social. With Betti and structuralism, Ricoeur emphasizes the importance and possibility of normative interpretation. At the same time, he criticizes any idea of a methodologically secured objective meaning as well as the exclusion by structuralism of the existential dimension of meaning.

24. R. Bultmann, "Das Problem der Hermeneutik," *Zeitschrift fur Philosophie und Kirche,* Vol. 47 (1950), p. 63.

25. Tracy, *op. cit.,* p. 51.

26. Heidegger, *op. cit.,* #32, p. 195.

27. Rosemary Ruether, *To Change the World* (New York: Crossroad Publishing, 1983), ch. 1, "Jesus and the Revolutionaries: Political Theology and Biblical Hermeneutics," p. 11.

28. Another telling example highlighting the impact of worldviews on exegesis is Al Wolters' "Nature and Grace in the Interpretation of Proverbs 31:10-31" in *Calvin Theological Journal* 19 (November, 1984), pp. 153-167.

29. Ricoeur also talks of three levels: the level of semantics, the level of reflection, and the existential level. Cf. his "Existence and Hermeneutics," in Bleicher, *op. cit.,* pp. 243-256.

30. Ricoeur, *Interpretation Theory,* pp. 74-79. In *Validity in Interpretation* (pp. 203-205), Hirsch identifies the "guess," the first act of intuitive understanding, and scientific "validation," the second act of understanding, with Schleiermacher's female "divinatory" function and male "comparative" function.

31. Ricoeur, "Existence and Hermeneutics," in Bleicher, *op. cit.,* p. 250.

32. Gerard Radnitzky, *Contemporary Schools of Metascience* (Chicago: Henry Regnery, 1968), p. 228.

33. The Critical Hermeneutics of Habermas and Apel as well as the more Marxian variants of Sandkühler and Lorenzer are incisively discussed by Bleicher, pp. 143-180. Bleicher includes a translation of one of Habermas' essays, "The Hermeneutic Claim to Universality," pp. 181-211. Cf. also Zygmunt Bauman, *Hermeneutics and Social Science Approaches to Understanding* (London: Hutchinson, 1978).

34. For the evangelical predilection for an intentionality theory of meaning, see Gerald Sheppard, "Biblical Hermeneutics: The Academic Language of Evangelical Identity," *Union Seminary Quarterly Review* 32 (1977), pp. 81-94.

35. Cf. Paul Ricoeur, "The Model of the Text: Meaningful Action Considered as a Text," *Social Research* 38 (1971), pp. 529-

541 and *Interpretation Theory: Discourse and Surplus of Meaning.*

36. Cf. Ricoeur, "Toward an Idea of the Hermeneutic of Revelation," *loc. cit.* Also Tracy, *op. cit.*, pp. 77-78.

37. Tracy, *op. cit.*, p. 76.

38. Ricoeur, *Interpretation Theory*, p. 43.

39. Fuchs, *Studies of the Historical Jesus* (London: SCM, 1964), pp. 196-98, and G. Ebeling, "Word of God and Hermeneutic," in *The New Hermeneutic*, pp. 78-110.

40. Gadamer, *op. cit.*, pp. 263 ff.

41. Richard Longenecker, "The 'Faith of Abraham' Theme in Paul, James and Hebrews: A Study in the Circumstantial Nature of New Testament Teaching," *Journal of the Evangelical Theological Society* 20 (1977), pp. 203-12.

42. See Walter Brueggemann, *The Creative Word* (Philadelphia: Fortress Press, 1982) for an excellent discussion of the nature of these three kinds of writings and their inter-relationships.

43. On Luke, cf. I. Howard Marshall, *The Gospel of Luke* (Grand Rapids: Eerdmans, 1974). For Mark, cf. William H. Lane, *The Gospel According to Mark* (Grand Rapids: Eerdmans, 1974). Robert Gundry has recently written a commentary, *Matthew: A Commentary on his Literary and Theological Art* (Grand Rapids: Eerdmans, 1982) which argues that it is appropriate to use the adjectives "midrashic" and "haggadic" for Matthew (cf. "A Theological Postscript," pp. 623-640).

44. Donald Sinnema, *Reclaiming the Land: A Study of the Book of Joshua* (Toronto: Joy in Learning Curriculum Centre, 1977), p. 8. Both Sinnema and Fernhout (cf. fn. 45) employ the certitudinal focus to advantage in their studies.

45. Cf. Harry Fernhout, *Of Kings and Prophets* (Toronto: Joy in Learning Curriculum Centre, 1979), p. 4. For I and II Samuel, cf. H. Fernhout, *Promises Broken; Promises Kept* (Toronto: Joy in Learning Curriculum Centre, 1986).

46. For the "literary program" of the Chronicler, see Raymond Dillard, "The Reign of Asa (2 Chronicles 14-16): An Example of the Chronicler's Theological Method," *Journal of the Evangelical Theological Society* 23 (1980), pp. 217-218.

47. Hans W. Frei has made a significant move to get beyond the dilemma by describing biblical narratives as "history-like" and pleading for a realistic, mimetic reading (*The Eclipse of Biblical Narrative* New Haven: Yale University Press, 1974, chap. 1). I am suggesting that we can make further headway by recognizing that the biblical narratives are history, history

written from the vantage point of faith-certitude.

48. I talk of "certitudinal" exegesis instead of "theological" because I want to honor the fact that certitudinal texts are not theo-logical, that is, theoretic texts, and their interpretation is not fundamentally or in the first place a theoretic endeavor. Moreover, the concept "theological" is itself highly ambiguous. Sometimes it means biblical teaching, sometimes systematically construed doctrines, sometimes the science of things divine, and sometimes the praxis of right living. Often it includes all of these and theological is used to indicate any reference to or any connection with God.

Theological interpretation is at times taken to mean God's way of interpreting or interpretation looked at from the viewpoint of an ideal observer such as God. I want to stress that looking at things from the viewpoint of faith certitudes is one completely human and natural way (alongside other modes of being human) which can be valid or invalid depending on its content. On the other hand, in much modern discussion, "theological" often indicates the subjective, constructive intention that we bring to the text. I want to emphasize that the focus on ultimate certitudes is a characteristic which is structurally built-in to the text of Scripture as a canonic whole regardless of the intentions of interpreters (or even some of the writers).

49. Calvin G. Seerveld has offered a helpful contrast between what I am calling a certitudinal reading of Numbers 22-24 with moralistic, higher-critical and orthodox intellectualistic readings in *Balaam's Apocalyptic Prophecies* (Toronto: Wedge Publishing Foundation, 1980). Sidney Greidanus has shown the inadequacy of a moralistic, exemplary approach in preaching historical texts in *Sola Scriptura: Problems and Principles in Preaching Historical Texts* (Toronto: Wedge Publishing Foundation, 1970), ch. 3.

50. In his commentary on II Timothy 3:16, John Calvin strongly emphasized the importance of *proper* use if the Scriptures are to fulfill their promise. Cf. *Commentaries on the Epistles to Timothy, Titus and Philemon* (Grand Rapids: Eerdmans, pp. 249-50.

51. For fuller treatments of such a biblical vision, cf. Brian J. Walsh and J. Richard Middleton, *The Transforming Vision* (Downer's Grove: InterVarsity Press, 1984) and Albert M. Wolters, *Creation Regained* (Grand Rapids: Eerdmans, 1985).

Peril with promise: a response to James Olthuis

by Clark H. Pinnock

Jesus gave us this warning: "Take heed how you hear" (Luke 8:18). James Olthuis is correct to insist on the importance of knowing how properly to interpret the Bible. For what profit is there if we profess a high doctrine of its authority and fail to interpret it correctly and profoundly? Authority is a functional category. It makes no sense to claim that Dr. Spock is my authority for child raising if I do not follow what he lays down. We must get a handle on biblical hermeneutics. Olthuis helps us to do so by integrating into a unique perspective his own many current insights. This essay carries further the theme of an earlier paper of his entitled "Towards a Certitudinal Hermeneutic" published in 1979 (*Hearing and Doing*, John Kraai and Anthony Tol, editors. Toronto: Wedge Publishing Foundation, pp. 65-85).

Olthuis is trying to renew evangelical thinking by creating some new space between old divisions in theology. I propose to pursue three lines of inquiry to uncover his ideas at greater depth. These do not exhaust the rich thinking in the paper, but may serve to help us reflect critically on it.

Does faith come through reason?

To my way of thinking the first topic he treats is ancillary to hermeneutics proper, although this may only reflect my own preference not to let the term include everything under the sun, as it tends to do today. Olthuis devotes some space to an explanation of how one arrives at the conviction that the Bible is the Word of God (pp. 12-16). Although this could be discussed in fundamental or apologetic theology or even in the psychology of belief, he raises it here because it is part of what he means by "certitudinal," that God gives us the assurance which we have concerning the truth of his revelation and Scripture. It does not come as the result of the efforts of human reason, but is given to us by grace. God discovers us; we do not discover Him. Convictions about ultimacy are not within the possibility of human reasoning, but appear in our consciousness as self-evident and self-authen-ticating.

It would take us too far afield to inquire how far Olthuis' thinking here lines up with traditional theology in its treatment of themes such as general revelation and the indicia of special revelation.

Lest we suppose, however, that Olthuis thinks faith is irra-tional, he introduces a number of disclaimers. It seems that there *are* reasons and evidences of all kinds in support of faith (14/15). Is it a self-evident conviction then or is it the final term in an exer-cise of apologetic reasoning? The answer comes in the form of a dis-tinction: "Fundamental acceptance does not come from reasons, although it may come through reasons." (15)

What can he possibly mean? I would venture to say that Olthuis sees reasoning as operating within a faith vision or perspective. Therefore believers can give reasons to themselves, but these reasons cannot be expected to be valid currency across faith perspectives. Arguments will not help anyone to adopt a faith vision, but they may help them once they have adopted it. Rational in this way of thinking is what I would call "internal" and not "external" rationality. As with Barth's so-called ratio-nal theology, reason operates within the circle of presupposed faith but not beyond it. Non-Christians could not expect to find arguments to convince them to adopt the Christian faith. When Olthuis says faith has "reasons," he means reasons believers will understand because they are established in the faith perspective, but they are not reasons which just anyone on common ground might be expected to accept. If this is so, I do not think he is being inconsistent in saying that faith is self-evident and that there are reasons for faith. I also think that according to the accepted definition of rationality — as reasoned thinking anyone could follow to a conclusion — Olthuis does not believe faith is rational.

At the same time, Olthuis is tempted to go further. He can even say: "Rational argumentation can only be the *means* by which, but not the *ground* on which a person accepts a new faith. Rational argument may occasion a change of faith, and may, in a fundamental way, urge the invalidity of a vision and its underlying faith." (16) What we ought to say is simply that, al-though the faith event is certainly a mystery, God who made the human mind can surely use the evidences of his activity and exis-tence to effect the conversion of the human heart. Even though the unbeliever may resist them, they remain valid evidences and need to be presented "whether they will hear or forbear." Why would a good Calvinist wish to even seem to restrict the divine freedom in this matter?

I suppose this is important for me in two ways. First, I do not like to hear Christian scholars telling unbelievers what they believe already, namely, that there will not be reasons why they should believe until they do believe. Contrary to what Paul says, they would seem to have the perfect excuse for never believing. Second, I do not like the smugness this allows the Christian community which can sweetly say: ""We believe (by grace of course); that settles it." Belief in this world settles nothing as far as the truth of religion is concerned. I tremble for the future of the Christian mission if we cannot go out into the market place of ideas convinced of the objective truthfulness of our message.

The vision of the text: reading within the macro-purpose

Olthuis keeps speaking about the vision we have of the Bible and the vision the Bible has of itself, and indicates how crucial it is for us to grasp these things. It is a matter we must pursue if it is of utmost importance for good interpretation. Let us start with the vision we bring to the text on account of our history and tradition (18).

Olthuis believes that we are shaped in our understanding of the Bible by the Christian tradition in which we stand. Evangelicals especially have not fully appreciated the way they engage the text in terms of the life vision they have received (35). We have tended to canonize our own understanding of the Bible and be closed to other understandings of it. We sometimes will say that we think of the Bible exactly the way in which it thinks about itself, and not be aware of traditional components in our thinking. Is Olthuis a relativist and a traditionalist, then? Does he agree with Kelsey (see 18) that each community or theologian decides how to approach the Bible and use it as an authority, and this is as it should be? There is nothing superior then about Warfield's approach over, say, Bultmann's or Tillich's. Or, I suppose, between Calvin's and Pope Innocent's. At this point Olthuis cites Carl Henry's review of Kelsey and issues a disclaimer, but his disagreement with Kelsey is by no means as clear as Henry's is. He does not actually say what Henry does, that the BIble has a "discrimen" for interpretation and it alone should be ours (in agreement with Warfield of course) and I am left wondering. It does not help to read (15) that no vision, such as a view of Scripture, is subject to proof, and I suppose to falsification. On the other hand, Olthuis says enough about the vision the Bible supposedly projects that he must be coming down at least softly on Henry's side.

Moving on then to the vision the text has of itself, we have to examine Olthuis' idea that there is a macro-purpose taught in the Bible which must direct our reading of it. This idea raises many intriguing questions. At once one wonders if — like the Scofield Bible notes — it will be a device to ensure that the reader will not fall into interpretations which disagree with the pre-set dogmatic system. After all, we are darkly warned that failure to understand the "structural specificity" of the text may result in its violation (22-26, 38f). This is evidently very serious business. What then is this vision, this macro-purpose? It is the theme of redemption that runs through the Bible, which unfolds the ways of God with men and women, and explains how we might live in a covenant relationship with him and be pleasing to him. It is a religious purpose, dealing with the dimension of ultimacy, but religious in the proper sense of addressing the whole of life "certitudinally."

I myself have little difficulty admitting that there is a basic message running through the Bible, but I should point out that many, perhaps most, biblical scholars would question it. The whole idea is reminiscent of the older biblical theology movement which sought to state Olthuis' central unified message (38). These scholars are greatly impressed by the theological diversity (one could call it contradictions) in the Bible, not only on the periphery where Olthuis might admit them, but in the center, too. Olthuis might try to handle them by his "analogy of Scripture" (40) which can always be counted on to eliminate disagreeable features in the text. But I will not press this further, because I think Olthuis can answer it to my satisfaction.

More serious would be the question whether in adopting a macro-purpose Olthuis is not skewing the text and channelling it into agreeable lines. Certainly the defenders of inerrancy will think so. Olthuis completely overthrows their position simply by definition. He informs us what kind of truth the Bible intends to teach according to its macro-purpose, and then can inform us triumphantly that the Bible has no errors by that standard (45). Bultmann of course could do the same. I can hear it now: "Statements about God are inerrant statements about man. No other so-called errors need disturb us." Olthuis makes the same move regarding inerrancy that Berkouwer and Fuller did before him. Simply define the purpose of the Bible more narrowly and the old errors can be granted without being called such. What makes it very interesting is that in effect it is only an extension of a principle in the older inerrancy thinking that the Bible is true in what it intends to teach, and presumably not necessarily true elsewhere. Olthuis hops through this gap brandishing his macro-purpose.

This leads us to a much deeper concern, and that has to do with exactly what sort of truth is contained in the macro-purpose as Olthuis understands it. It is not just a question of what to do with an inaccurate king list in Chronicles, but with what kind of biblical truth *is* binding on us. The same question comes up in respect of Berkouwer. Once theologians start to talk mysteriously about truth being "functional" and the text being "encountered," as Olthuis repeatedly does, you have to ask yourself what you are supposed to believe then. I could fill the page with phrases he uses that sound as if one does not need to believe the information the Bible gives so long as he gets to know God better. Apparently we do not need to share Paul's views or opinions (31). It is rather a question of communion with the text (27). We should not think of the Bible as a deposit of propositional truths to be mined for reliable information (28). The truth is functional (19). The sentences are certitudinally qualified (44). The content is taken up into the focus on the ultimate (44). Scripture is true at a depth-level (45). Now one cannot continue to talk like this and not expect to give the impression, not to say certainty, that the theologian takes the truth of the Bible to be symbolic and existential and not literal and ontological. Now the question is far more serious. It is not just a matter of a doctrinal core being true amid a lot of uncertain periphery, but whether there is even a doctrinal core at all. We recall Cullmann saying that New Testament Christology was functional, too, by which he meant that it referred to what Christ did and not who Christ was. Is this what certitudinal hermeneutics also does? Olthuis must clarify where he stands over against the school of existentialist theologians.

The problem with having a macro-purpose is that it can silence the text rather than open it up. If the macro-purpose is in any way woven out of contemporary philosophical cloth, it will allow the interpreter to twist the Scriptures. Ironically Olthuis claims that without a proper macro-purpose one will inevitably violate the text (22). He ought to add that with the wrong one one is certain to violate it. It will inevitably corrupt and not in any way assist our reading of Scripture.

My problem with certitudinal hermeneutics is that it is so vague. I cannot predict the results it will produce when actually applied to the text. I sense it will require much less of us when it comes to believing aspects of the Scripture like factual matters, but I am not at all certain if it requires me to believe such things as Adam's historical fall or Satan's actual existence. And because it is vague I even suspect it will do different things for different practitioners when Olthuis is out of earshot. You see, I am not as confident as he seems to be that most Christians are eager to submit to the divine authority of the Bible (11). I see a good deal of what I would consider Scripture twisting and Bible denying going on. I take the New Testament seriously when it warns that Satan is in the business of deceiving the church, and think we cannot be too careful being clear and forthright in a matter as crucial as hermeneutics.

Before moving on, I ought to refer to the unseen presence in all of this of Dooyeweerd's philosophy. It is kept discreetly under wraps, but eventually the reader of Olthuis pieces things together in its light. The very term "certitudinal" is a code word to refer to the so-called pistic modal aspect of reality in that system of thought. (One must be prepared for a whole new vocabulary!) The Bible addresses directly only this modal aspect, the realm of faith and certitude (34). When it seems to address other spheres we must remember to qualify what it says "certitudinally," that is, pistically. The authority of the Bible is thus greatly restricted in the other fourteen modal aspects in the system. We need not seek proof texts for them (45). We apply the Bible dynamically in those regions (45). How does it work then? As Olthuis replied to Frame in 1975, we take the biblical directives to heart and "act in that same radical manner" (*Vanguard*, January 1975, p. 11). Such an approach seems to leave a good deal of leeway for the reader of the Bible to do his own thing. Since the moral modal aspect is different from the pistic aspect, do the biblical moral directives not apply directly to the moral aspect, then? It seems to me that although the role of a modern philosophy is not acknowledged, Dooyeweerd's thinking is operating magisterially here, and the Bible is being given the place that system permits it to have. Its authority is restricted from the start to the pigeon hole allotted to it. This is reminiscent of the role Heidegger's categories play in Bultmann's work.

Another area where Olthuis confuses me is in his denial of the possibility and desirability of the objective exegesis of Scripture (26-28). From other remarks of his, I do not think he can mean what he seems to say, that we ought not to suppose we can attain an objective reading of the text. After all, he says the Bible can at times be completely clear (21). It makes its own structural specificity fully known (23). The first level in hermeneutics is precisely ascertaining the sense of the text (33). He even advises us how to attain it (19-22, 37-42).

What then can he mean when he tells us that objectivity is an illusion, based as it is on a discredited concept of subject and object, stemming from Descartes (26-28)? Perhaps he only means that total objectivity is practically impossible, and that we have to be self-critical in regard to the pre-understandings we bring with us to the text. But the way he words it makes it sound as if he actually denies that an objective reading of the Bible is what we ought to be striving for. And it does not help to cite Bultmann in an attempt to assure us that the text can correct us, too, since he allows it to do so only to a limited extent (29).

The roots of this subjectivist tendency must also lie in the Dooyeweerdian system which allows the appearance of objective thinking in naive experience and distinguishes that sharply from theoretical thought. This nuance would seem to leave somewhat incapacitated the power of the Bible to teach us in the latter realm.

Even to appear to deny the ideal of an objective reading of the text is to open interpretation up to radical subjectivism. If the text cannot speak its own mind, the interpreter of it has the golden opportunity to speak its mind for it, and the result will almost inevitably be more of the same theological revision we have been seeing in the liberal camp. We ought to be saying that even though totally objective and presuppositionless exegesis is impossible, an objective reading of the text is what we should always strive for. Otherwise what will happen is that interpreters will impose upon it notions they derive from their culture and opinions, and the task of true hermeneutics is doomed from the start. In my judgment, the Christian community is in constant danger of being assimilated into the secular vortex. The Bible stands as the strongest single obstacle in the way of this happening. Once its ability to speak its message objectively above the noise of human opinions is compromised, it will no longer be able to prevent the assimilation, and enculturation will accelerate tenfold.

Conclusion

Is Olthuis a reliable guide to the interpretation of the Bible? I cannot say that he is. It may be that he will be able to clear away my doubts about what he is saying. But at this point hesitations are aroused. He leaves hermeneutics far too vague and undefined, and seems even to allow it to be shaped by a chosen philosophical structure. In doing this, Olthuis is part of the problem of hermeneutics today, rather than an evangelical corrective to it. Clarification and qualification will, I think, be necessary before certitudinal hermeneutics will bear much good fruit.

Promise with peril: a response to James Olthuis

by Donald G. Bloesch

Points of convergence and divergence

After reading the paper by James Olthuis, I felt encouraged but also disquieted. Could this be an attempt to bind the Holy Spirit to a hermeneutical method, or does this represent a Reformed and ipso facto evangelical critique of the new hermeneutic?

On the whole, I feel very much at home with the main thrust of this paper. With the author, I affirm that the Bible is self-authenticating and that external evidences and arguments can be aids in understanding the truth of faith but not tangible or unambiguous proofs.

I also agree with his definitions of truth and error. He rightly reminds us that truth in Scripture generally signifies faithfulness rather than scientific precision and that error indicates instability or deception, not defective information. One can say that truth in the biblical perspective is the redemptively transformable rather than the empirically verifiable (as in naturalism) or the rationally inescapable (as in idealism).

Moreover, I concur in his judgment that the uncovering of authorial intention is not yet understanding or interpretation. He is also sound in his view that the object of interpretation is not the intention of the author or the existential moment of decision but the text itself.

Finally, I warmly endorse his contention that no amount of scientific-historical investigation can decide the basic question of Scriptural authority. Historical and literary criticism can throw light upon the cultural background of the text and redaction criticism can tell us many things about the author, but none of these can determine the authority that the text should have in the church of today.

This paper raises a number of questions, however. First, I am somewhat perplexed by Olthuis' appeal to the "vision of the text." If this means the worldview of the author of the text, then I must take exception, since the biblical message must not be confused with a particular *Weltanschauung.* On the other hand, if it means the way in which the text is related to the self-revelation of God in Jesus Christ, the culminating point of biblical salvation history, then it is much more acceptable.

Olthuis sees biblical authority as experiential and functional, but is it not ontological as well? If Scripture is a product of the inspiration of the Spirit of God (II Tim. 3:16), if the Spirit is the primary author and the elected servants of God secondary authors, then surely Scripture has an ontological basis, for it is grounded in the very wisdom and knowledge of God. Moreover, since the Spirit preserves Scripture from dissolution and maintains the integrity of the witness of Scripture, it can be surmised that Scripture participates in the divine reality which is its source.

Again, Olthuis suggests that a primary aim of the text is to transform the self-understanding of the interpreter (26). He here shows his kinship to existentialist philosophy and theolo-gy, which sees the language of Scripture as a vehicle for understanding human existence rather than a source of information about God. My question is this: Is not the fundamental intention of the text to lead us to a saving knowledge of Jesus Christ? Olthuis does allude to the "redemptive intention" of the text, but the question remains whether this is redemption understood as an encounter with Being (à la Heidegger) or redemption understood as deliverance through what God has done objectively in the Jesus Christ of history. I believe that Olthuis would lean toward the latter, but he is not always clear on this point.

I cannot escape the feeling that a preoccupation with a fully reliable hermeneutical method flirts with the danger of Gnosticism, which reserves knowledge of the truth to an intellectual or spiritual elite. Olthuis is right that "every text needs interpretation in order to be understood" (19), but he relies much more, it seems, on the input from an array of experts (21) than on the theological commentary on Scripture in the tradition of the church.

This brings us to his contention that we are led to confess our faith in terms of a vision of life which we bring to the text but which is also supposedly drawn from Scripture (15, 16). The danger here is that an a priori philosophical schema may become the real authority rather than the message of the Bible. Olthuis re-establishes his Reformed credentials when he acknowledges that faith itself supplies a vision of life which "integrates and leads our daily walk of life" (25).

I would have liked more clarification concerning the meaning of revelation, especially the way in which it is related to Holy Scripture. Olthuis tends to accept Gilkey's definition of revelation as "that definite mode of experience in which a particular answer" is given to the "ultimate questions that arise in all secular life" (13). This definition harmonizes with Tillich's understanding of revelation, but is it biblical? Is not revelation, as the Bible conceives it, God's intervention into human experience rather than "a mode of experience"? Does not revelation consist in God's act of self-disclosure that breaks into our experience and transforms our experience? Surely God's self-revelation cuts the ground from under our creative questions rather than simply answering them (as in Tillich's method of correlation). Is revelation universal in human existence, as Gilkey maintains, or particular in human history? One can perhaps speak of a general revelation, but the light that it conveys is only a reflection of the one great light that is Jesus Christ, and we cannot really understand these little lights except from the vantage point of God's self-revelation in Christ (Barth).

Olthuis follows existentialist theology and the new hermeneutic in separating faith and cognitive knowing (16). But does not faith itself bring us knowledge of God and of his saving work in Jesus Christ? Is not faith, as Calvin said, "a steady and certain knowledge" of the will and purpose of God toward us?

The role of hermeneutics
I agree with Karl Barth that hermeneutical principles should not be derived from general reflections on the nature of human language or existence, i.e., from a general anthropology.[1] At the same time, the hermeneutical guidelines that we derive from revelation should inform the way we assess truth claims in general as we find these in philosophy and other religions. Olthuis is not always consistent, but it seems that he begins with the Word addressing us and then guiding us in our interpretation. On the other hand, he accepts the position of the new hermeneutic that we need to come to the text with what Bultmann calls a pre-understanding (*Vorverständnis*) that will guide us in our interpretation. His qualification is that this pre-understanding should itself be derived from revelation.

Olthuis is sound in his asseveration that a presuppositionless exegesis is an illusion. Even Barth recognized that we can never escape from our pre-suppositions entirely and that we must always seek to be very much aware of them, especially in the task of interpreting Scripture. Yet a distinction must be made between the *fact* of preconceptions and the *need* for such preconceptions. It is my belief that a preunderstanding more often than not stands in the way of the authentic understanding of the text rather than facilitating it. This is because there will always be an infinite qualitative difference between God and humanity, even redeemed humanity (cf. Isa. 55:8; Hos. 11:9). Barth, in my opinion, is on firm ground when he argues that we should endeavor always to come to Scripture without any overt presuppositions or at least with the intention of bringing these presuppositions under the judgment of the Word of God. Berkouwer is also keenly aware of the hermeneutical temptation of making the text conform to a priori speculation. His emphasis is on "listening" to the text rather than imposing upon it an a priori logical schema.[2]

Olthuis nowhere appeals either to Barth or to Berkouwer, but he does give much attention to existentialists and philosophical thinkers such as Polanyi who speak of the need for a tacit reliance on a conceptual system in the task of interpretation. In my position the norm for faith is given by the Spirit in a free and new act of disclosure as we encounter the text in a spirit of openness that characterizes faith. This "dogmatic norm" will always exist in tension with our pre-understanding and even overthrow it. Olthuis makes a place for this, but he appears to view the pre-understanding in a positive more than a negative light.

I share with Barth a concern to safeguard the freedom of the Word of God. The truth or meaning of the Word is never there at our disposal even when we use the correct hermeneutical procedures. God's Word can be heard only when God speaks, and God may speak his Word over and against our human searching and reading of Scripture. God may also choose to withhold his Word, and no amount of hermeneutical dexterity can procure the truth of revelation in these circumstances.

Against the stream of interpretation flowing from Schleier-macher, Olthuis insists that it is not a psychological disposition that we share with the author of the text but rather a vision of life. I contend that we do not necessarily even share this if we mean by it a life- and world-view. What we share is a relationship to Jesus Christ that only the Spirit can reveal and make clear. One may perhaps speak of a biblical view of God, man and the world, but this is only an overall perspective that is gleaned from Scripture as a whole and may not be necessarily held by every Scriptural author (certainly not the writer of Ecclesiastes).

Olthuis follows the new hermeneutic in affirming the reality of the hermeneutical circle in which we argue from the text to the whole of Scripture and then back to the perspective of faith. I agree that a biblical hermeneutic will take a circular form, but I contend (with Berkouwer) that the truth of revelation breaks into this hermeneutical circle, or otherwise it remains unknown. Revelation is not a truth simply available to human perception or conception; it is an event that takes place when God acts through the power of his Spirit — not only in the text but in our hearts, and this event then transforms our perceptions and conceptions.

Olthuis speaks of the aim of hermeneutics as the objective reproduction of the author's vision or world-view (39), which is supposedly fixed in the text (39). Is it not rather the discerning of the Spirit's intention as he speaks to us now through the text? This is not pneumatic exegesis, since the Spirit does not bypass the text and speak directly to us. It is closer to what Barth calls "theological exegesis" — trying to find with the aid of the Spirit the relation of the text to Jesus Christ, his life, death and resurrection.

This brings us to the question of the principal focus of Scripture. Olthuis is convinced that the "governing focus" of Scripture is "the ultimate questions of life and death" (24). The aim of Scripture is to give certitudinal knowledge of the answers to life's fundamental questions. Here Olthuis sees the bridge or correlation between philosophy and theology. I hold that the central focus of Scripture is the proclamation of God's act of reconciliation and redemption in Jesus Christ. This proclamation has metaphysical implications, but it is not so much a life- and world-view as a report of the saving deeds of God in the biblical history culminating in Jesus Christ.

Olthuis proposes a "certitudinal-grammatical-historical exegesis" for both the historico-critical method of the higher critics and the traditional grammatical-historical method of the lower critics. I see his exegesis as supplementing traditional methods by a philosophical hermeneutic. In place of all these, I propose a theological exegesis that gives assurance of salvation and insight into the plan of salvation but not necessarily definite answers to all of life's ultimate questions, at least as these are envisioned by philosophers. At the same time, I believe that the biblical answers throw light on philosophical questions, and perhaps here I am not far from Olthuis.

The author describes the vision of life as the "spectacles" through which we make sense of life. He is here thinking basically of a life- and world-view. I see Jesus Christ himself as the spectacles by which we make sense of life, the Christ who enters into our modes of cognition and brings them into his service. Paul claimed to have "the mind of Christ" (I Cor. 2:16), not a superior view of the world or a more sophisticated anthropology.

Whereas Olthuis puts the accent on the vision of life, which guides us in understanding the text, I see the Bible as focusing on the obedience of faith apart from which the text will remain veiled to us. I perceive the biblical concern as being more ethical than certitudinal, more evangelistic than hermeneutical. Our vocation, after all, is not to be interpreters of mysteries but to be witnesses to the meaning that shines through mystery for all who believe.

Evangelical or existentialist hermeneutics?
Olthuis is to be commended for opening up a dialogue between the Reformed tradition and the new hermeneutic. He demonstrates that he is willing to learn from the new philosophical understandings of meaning and language. His commitment to the biblical faith is unassailable, but the question remains whether he depends too heavily on existentialist thought in his construction of a biblical hermeneutic.

There is peril as well as promise in this kind of enterprise. Existentialism in one or more of its expressions has been of substantial aid to the dialectical theology of Karl Barth and Emil Brunner as well as to the neo-liberal theology of Bultmann and Tillich. Existentialist philosophy has reminded theology that ideas apart from personal appropriation remain empty and abstract. When existentialism is allowed to dictate the agenda for theology, however, theology is reduced to anthropology, the historical is sacrificed to the experiential.

Heidegger's philosophy in particular has proved a pervasive influence on the new hermeneutic. For both Bultmann and Tillich, modern existentialist philosophy gives an accurate diagnosis of human existence and therefore points to the Christian answer given in revelation. The trouble with this is that Heidegger's philosophy and not the Old Testament becomes the propaedeutic to New Testament theology. Existentialist theologians definitely devalue the Old Testament; at the most it is a questionable preamble to the New Testament.

The disjunction between existence and thought, faith and knowledge, is one of the premises of existentialism. We have seen this to some extent in Olthuis' paper, though he has also expressed ideas that go counter to this position. Olthuis concurs in the judgment of Ebeling and Gadamer that we do not understand words but we understand through words (22). The question is: What do we understand? Olthuis reflects the thought-world of existentialism when he says that we are led to a new self-understanding through an encounter with the text (26). But does not the text also give us information about God, humanity and the world? In Christian existentialism the word is seen in terms of formative power rather than informative statement, and faith becomes decision or resolution. According to Ernst Fuchs, the language-event (*Sprachereignis*) which takes place in the New Testament signifies not the communication of concepts but a call (*Berufung*) or a pledge (*Einsatz*).[3] But does not this empty revelation of its conceptual or propositional content?[4]

Olthuis holds that the words of the Bible point beyond themselves to a "non-semantic" reality (22). Does this mean that they also refer to non-rational or non-cognitive reality? The slippery slope that leads from existentialism to a monistic mysticism is too readily apparent among both Christian and nonchristian existentialists. Olthuis guards against this by seeking to hold on to an objective revelation given in Holy Scripture.

He also empathizes with the existentialist critique of Cartesianism and with the existentialist attempt to transcend the subject-object dichotomy. If this means trying to get beyond the self-world polarity and even beyond the divine-human encounter where all distinctions are lost in an undifferentiated unity or in some all-encompassing creative force, then again we are closer to mysticism than to biblical faith. On the other hand, if our aim is fellowship between the I and the Thou in which external relations are transfigured rather than overcome, then this kind of concern is not out of harmony with the claims of biblical faith.

Evangelical theology, as exemplified in Calvin, Luther and Barth, begins not from general human experience or even from religious experience but from a definitive, historical revelation. It then seeks to understand the totality of experience in the light of this revelation. In the early part of his paper, Olthuis appears to begin with a general experience of ultimacy and then proceeds to relate this to the Christian faith (16). He is nevertheless very close to the Reformation stance when he insists that only by revelation can we enter the hermeneutical circle and that our pre-understanding must be drawn from revelation.

In evangelical theology what we experience through the hearing of the gospel is conviction of sin and the love and grace of

Jesus Christ. In existentialism what we experience through the language of poetic inspiration (including biblical language) is the wonder of Being (Heidegger) or a deeper insight into ourselves. Evangelical theology is oriented about a particular revelation in history which gives meaning to the whole of life; existentialism on the other hand is oriented about the human predicament of living in a meaningless world.

There are two erroneous ways of approaching the Bible. The first is to bring our own meanings to the Scripture, which amounts to reading into Scripture personal biases instead of finding what is really God's word for us. This is the way of existentialist and neo-liberal theologies. The second questionable method is to suppose that the words of Scripture contain their own meanings, which implies that the truth of the Word of God is self-evident. This is the approach of Protestant scholastic orthodoxy and fundamentalism. The better way is to allow ourselves to be grasped by the meaning that God's Spirit gives to the text as it is seen in its wider context, that is to say, in the light of the cross of Christ. In this view, the meaning of the text is revealed rather than assumed or simply discovered. This reflects the stance of original evangelicalism.

The new hermeneutic correctly asks: How can God's word "which once took the form of human speech in a given time and place be understood and translated without abridgement of power and meaning into a different time and place"?[5] The solution propounded by those under the spell of existentialism is to enter into the same kind of experience as the author of the text in question. But this means that the focus of attention is on the inwardness of the author rather than the objective meaning of the text. Olthuis is alive to this peril, and this is why he stresses the vision of the text over both the intention and the experience of the author as the object of the hermeneutical quest. I would prefer to focus attention on God's decisive intervention into history in the person of Jesus Christ and then try to understand how every biblical text is related to this supreme event in history.

Carl Braaten suggests that the hermeneutical bridge that spans the wide chasm between biblical-salvation history and contemporary history is not the history of language or the language event as such but the history of the people of God, the history of the ecclesia which is an ongoing part of salvation-history.[6] I would rather say that it is the work of the Spirit of God as he dwells within but also acts upon the church enabling people of every age to appropriate the fruits of the cross and resurrection of Christ.[7] The key to an evangelical hermeneutic is not even the church as such but the event of redemption in Jesus Christ whose power and impact are conveyed to people of every age by the rekindling of the reality of Pentecost.

NOTES

1. Karl Barth, *Church Dogmatics* I, w. Eds. G. W. Bromiley & T. F. Torrance. (Edinburgh: T. & T. Clark, 1956), pp. 465-472.

2. See G. C. Berkouwer, *Holy Scripture* trans. and ed. Jack Rogers (Grand Rapids: Eerdmans, 1975), pp. 105-138. Also see Gary Wynn Watts, *The Theological Method of G. C. Berkouwer* (Pasadena, Calif: Fuller Theological Seminary Ph. D. Thesis, 1981), pp. 261-281.

3. See Ernst Fuchs, *Studies of the Historical Jesus* trans. Andrew Scobie (London: SCM, 1964), pp. 94, 95.

4. For a timely evangelical critique of existentialist hermeneutics see Anthony C. Thiselton, *The Two Horizons* (Grand Rapids: Wm. B. Eerdmans, 1980), pp. 327-356. Also see Amos Wilder, "The Word as Address and the Word as Meaning" in James M. Robinson and John B. Cobb, Jr. *The New Hermeneutic* (New York: Harper & Row, 1964), pp. 198-218.

5. Carl Braaten, "How New is the New Hermeneutic?" in *Theology Today*, Vol. XXII, No. 2 (July, 1965), [218-235], p. 227.

6. *Ibid.*, p. 233.

7. In amplifying his position Braaten comes very close to my own, since he also sees the work of the Spirit in the church as crucial for merging the horizons of the biblical authors and modern readers.

A promising synthesis

by Gerald T. Sheppard

The genius of this essay lies not so much in the originality of its hermeneutical ideas about the Bible as in its impressive drive toward a radically new synthesis between the concerns of self-styled "evangelicals" in the North American context and the post-modern proposals emerging internationally in Western philosophy and culture. In taking this direction, I believe the essay is prophetic insofar as it points in a constructive direction that evangelicals could move if they have imagination and nerve. However, this essay may illustrate just how political rather than grandly intellectual are the differences between Christian groups when they seek to discuss the Scripture they allegedly hold in common. If for some this essay "falls between the stools," we should at least ask why they cannot sit down at such a feast of ideas.

For these reasons, I want to risk a brief "economic" scenario in which I would place Olthuis' essay, then move to my own appreciation and criticism. From my own biased perspective, "fundamentalism" and "liberalism" in America and in some Canadian groups were options which invested in the same general conception of modernity. Therefore, the terms of "objectivity" in the conflict between these two opponents were essentially the same, and, in my opinion, left wing liberalism deservedly won the major intellectual and institutional battles of the 1920's and 1930's. In Canada, the situation has been more complicated and the American fundamentalist formula of wedding a crude right wing modernist defense of orthodoxy with a historicist dispensationalism did not gain the same hold on the public imagination. In any case, in America this combination quickly galvanized disparate groups into a powerful political movement, which has only recently attained its greatest strength and public acceptance. At a very high level of generality, I would argue that following the 1930's in North America we saw the maturation of the confessional offspring from these divorced parents manifest in a "lower culture" evangelical movement and its "neo-orthodox" counterpoint rooted more firmly in Western "higher culture." In that period, class distinctions between denominations (with the exception of black church participants) vividly distinguished the "historic" denominations which predominated in the established, neo-orthodox seminaries from the "free church" denominations which were more commonly found in the newer "evangelical" Bible colleges and seminaries.

These rough economic and political lines of division have since the 1960's steadily eroded — so much so that today the separate "evangelical seminaries" now appear to have become centers of a conservative "neo-orthodoxy" just as the erstwhile "liberal" or "neo-orthodox" seminaries have moved toward confessional forms of liberation theology. With the collapse of an older consensus regarding modernity in both camps, one now senses an escalating crisis in identity, with its inevitable threat from once dependable sources of economic support for these seminaries. At present we see increasing strength among what I would call "charismatic fundamentalists" (e.g., Jerry Falwell and "fundamentalist" pentecostal-charismatics like Pat Robertson) whose enemy is secular humanism in the world more than liberalism in the churches. In contrast, both evangelicalism and neo-orthodoxy have lost their vitality as movements in the churches. Evangelicals betray their disarray by an overly nuanced effort to retain the label (e. g., "neo-," "young-," "radical-," or "conservative" evangelicals), while in contradiction to their Social Gospel heritage the once "liberal" or "neo-orthodox" groups have succumbed to describing themselves as "mainline" or "mainstream." The latter label offers only an uninspired assurance that these churches are not "sectarian" or marginal to the prevailing culture. Within this context, Olthuis' essay is a bold attempt to help evangelicals find a new hermeneutical identity which will treasure what is most important and stake out its own special place in a postmodern world. The implications are at once inherently political as much as they are theological.

This scenario is perhaps not so vivid in Canada as in the United States, but many of the Dutch Reformed in Canada, in which Olthuis finds rootage, have contributed to the culturally independent American and British "evangelicals" as co-conspirators. The intellectual depth of the Dutch Reformed tradition — with such towering figures as Kuyper, Dooyeweerd, and Bavinck — has provided an impressive corrective within evangelical circles based on a superior understanding of the relationship

between culture, philosophy, and social ethics. Olthuis' essay
continues that tradition by conversing on the one hand with well-
known philosophical-hermeneutical figures (e.g., Schleiermacher, Ricoeur, Gadamer, Polanyi), and on the other hand with
much lesser known, "evangelical" theologians (e.g., Buswell,
Carnell, Montgomery, Pinnock, Henry, Clark). This attempt risks
losing an audience outside of politicized evangelical circles. As an
intellectually rigorous act of pastoral care, Olthuis' essay de-
serves far more appreciation than it is likely to receive from
either side.

As an observer from outside of the narrowly defined "evangelical" controversy, I see two outstanding contributions in Olthuis'
essay. First, he rejects the commonplace evangelical attempt to
define the meaning of a text strictly in terms of authorial intent.
Second, he tries to describe how the biblical traditions form in
Scripture a peculiar kind of text, distinguishable from other types
of literature and inviting a search for a specialized "method of
Scripture interpretation."

In the past, fundamentalist and evangelical disputes over
Scripture have usually been expressed as struggles over how to
relate the "intents" of biblical authors or redactors to the unified
message of the Bible, read as a book of divine revelation.
Allowing for some "accommodation" of the intents of biblical
authors, evangelicals disputed one another in nuanced debates
over the relation of inspiration to revelation and how an intent
could be inerrant and/or infallible. Scofield could, for instance,
argue that by inspiration the words of Solomon were precisely
preserved in Ecclesiastes, then assure his readers that they were
as "non-revelatory" as the infallibly preserved words of the
serpent in the Garden of Eden or those of Satan in the prologue to
Job. Evangelicals, also, have hotly debated what part of an
author's intent might be infallible ("in matters of faith and
practice") or whether a philosophically more refined theory of
intentionality might itself be able to secure how the Bible is
"inerrant in all that it affirms." Historical criticism could only be
tolerated when thoroughly domesticated by "evangelical
presuppositions." Olthuis breaks entirely out of this debate with
claims like, "*What* the text says matters now much more than
what the author meant to say." Concomitantly, he rejects even
the most sophisticated *non*-evangelical defenses for a strict
intentionality theory of meaning (e.g., Betti, Hirsch). Nevertheless, Olthuis thinks knowledge of authors' intents "...and extra-
textual determinates are important." For that reason he can

affirm that "historical criticism is invaluable." Regarding *how* authors' intentions are important in biblical interpretation, Olthuis simply admits that this matter "still requires much work."

I believe Olthuis has correctly shifted evangelical attention to more fundamental matters and sought to bracket the issue of intentionality as only one issue among others in a more fruitful deliberation over, for example, the role that historical reference should play within the theological interpretation of a scriptural text. He shows that the more significant confessional claims of evangelicals have been hindered rather than helped by the attempt to ground evangelical claims on a precarious (and thoroughly modern) theory of intentionality. As a historical critic, I would argue further that the actual nature of the edited texts in the Bible rules out *prima facie* any appeal to the intent of a single human author for most individual books, much less for the Bible as a whole. If one wants to read a biblical book, a modern appeal to authorial intent almost always functions dialectically. It contributes somewhat to our understanding of the biblical text and, at the same time, focuses the object of interpretation no longer explicitly on the biblical text but on some historically reconstructed pretext. Olthuis has articulately suggested his own modification of Paul Ricoeur's proposal about meaning appearing in front of a text rather than residing within it as a "past tense," gleaned through speculation about what may have once constituted an author's "original" intent. Consequently, Olthuis offers a profound way to begin to address these issues beyond the older modernist posturing of the hermeneutical question.

The second area of great appreciation relates to how Olthuis freshly challenges us to re-consider just what type of literature the Bible is. Contemporary proposals that encourage us to read the Bible "as literature" or "like any other book" can appear condescendingly trite, if not tautological. After all, the Bible is obviously "literature"; how else could it be *read*? It may be the book of books but, regardless, no book is read exactly like every other book. While John Calvin, with his French humanist training, granted that "the style of some of the prophets is not sur-knowledged that much of the Bible bears marks of "a rude and homely style." Olthuis perceives that the Bible's uniqueness lies not in its aesthetic excellence but in its unusual claim upon readers as a "certitudinal text," belonging to a class of books often called "sacred texts." He finds support for this view in Childs' and my work, which I think is correct. I suspect that Olthuis' term "certitudinal" results from a concession to the evangelical pre-occupation with "authority" and "propositional" revelation.   I would prefer more simply "scriptural texts," and then see more discussion of two matters: how such texts have some features in common as a distinct "type of literature" (helped by compara-tivists such as Mircea Eliade, W. C. Smith, or F. Peters), and how Christian Scripture historically achieves its own distinct charac-teristics (cf. Childs, R. Rendtorff, and J. Sanders). With more such control I believe that Olthuis could press his case further. I think that he is on the right track and, through a more rigorous speci-fication of this type of literature, could go even further to help us understand how the Bible provides a normative arena for our theological reflection.   More critical assessment by Olthuis of what other non-evangelical scholars have already begun to do in this regard would be enormously helpful.

Since two other respondents have preceded me, I will limit my criticisms of Olthuis' essay to one general observation and one specific comment. What this essay needs is careful treatment of more biblical texts and more conversation with significant secon-dary literature. This is only another instance of the amazing gulf that seems to exist these days between theologians or philo-sophers of religion and biblical scholars. Perhaps biblical theo-logians have deserved their isolation in part by their choosing — at the height of the Biblical Theology Movement — to limit the aim of their work to stating what the Bible "meant" so that theologians could subsequently say what the Bible "means." This separation of biblical studies from philosophical theology also means that too many evangelical biblical scholars will probably find Olthuis' insights too "abstract." There is clearly a need for a better exchange between biblical and theological colleagues, re-gardless of their affiliation.

My one specific comment is that the opening section stresses the necessity of "revelation" in order to justify the prior conditions for a reasoned belief in God and a confidence that Scripture should be read as the normative text of Christian theology.   Olthuis seems to agree with Gilkey that such revelation "is universal in human existence." Of course, Wittgenstein would not consent to the idea that "the scaffolding of thought" should be called "reve-lation," any more than Gödel's incompleteness theorem need sug-gest that one should look for divine guidance. Therefore, I would want to distinguish sharply between "revelation" as a universal principle of human existence and the more historically specific claim that God through the power of the Holy Spirit has revealed something about Scripture to us. I think that John Cal-vin appeals to the latter and not the former. As Olthuis knows, Calvin defends his reliance on Scripture by an appeal to the Holy Spirit and "the conviction which revelation from heaven alone can produce." It is just such a clumsy and pragmatic assertion, fraught at the outset with anxieties of self-deception and uncrit-ical piety, that makes Christian theology so politically adven-turist. As reflective-action ever tempted by the demonic, it is far more dangerous than the effort to master a "language game." Olthuis could spell out more clearly how the existential require-ment of some "faith" in order to live in the world relates to reve-lation by the Holy Spirit that Scripture provides a sufficient wit-ness to God's special revelation in history.

Regardless, Olthuis has pointed impressively to a new way for evangelicals to engage these issues, realizing that the issues themselves can, in the end, never be reduced to matters of compe-tent syntactical exegesis but must be elevated, however awk-wardly, to decisions about life and death.

Peril or promise:
a reply

By James H. Olthuis

Clark Pinnock and Donald Bloesch see peril and promise in my effort to develop a hermeneutic approach to Scripture, Bloesch more promise and Pinnock more peril. Gerald Sheppard believes that my essay prophetically points in a constructive direction. Before replying to some of the issues which they raise, I want to express my deep appreciation for their responses. What we need most of all in our efforts to make headway in the important and complex arena of Scripture interpretation is congenial, interdisciplinary discussion and teamwork among colleagues in biblical studies, theology, philosophy, psychology, history, linguistics, and the social sciences. I hope that my reply to a number of issues raised by my critics will serve to continue the discussion.

Hermeneutics
Clark Pinnock wonders out loud why I would begin my hermeneutic proposal with a discussion of biblical authority. That topic, in his view, is ancillary to hermeneutics proper. In a discussion of general hermeneutics that would indeed be the case. However, for a biblical hermeneutic, paying attention to the status of the text to be interpreted is especially crucial.

In our context two special features make some treatment of biblical authority highly desirable. In the first place a fair number of evangelicals still see hermeneutics as a cloak for the denial of Scripture. Secondly, I want at the outset to distance myself from those who see hermeneutics as the way to determine and create meaning. Hermeneutics, as the science of interpretation, does not, in my view, create meaning: it helps unpack, unfold, and tease out the meaning (or lack of meaning) that is intrinsic to life in God's good (but fallen) creation.

Specifically, in reference to Scripture, hermeneutics does not, as integral to its task, decide the legitimacy of the biblical claim to be the Canon for life. However, it can be of considerable help as we strive to improve, deepen, and enrich our reading of Scripture as that Canon.

Reason and faith

The place of reason in coming to faith and in accepting Scripture as Canon for life has, of course, been widely debated — and still is. Pinnock judges that I underplay the role of reason and that I do not believe that faith is rational.

Pinnock correctly observes that I see reason as being operative within a faith vision or perspective. He is mistaken, however, in concluding that for me "reasons cannot be expected to be valid currency across faith perspectives." Implicit in my acceptance of valid reasons is my conviction that they ought to be compelling for everyone. If the reasons convince me, why shouldn't they convince others? If they are merely reasons, what is their compelling reasonableness? What we accept to be most true for ourselves we also believe to be the universal pattern for all of life.

Thus, I do insist, along with Pinnock, that there are reasons why people "should believe before they believe." My contention is, however, that the reasons only become compelling for a specific individual when that person, in God's grace, surrenders his/her life to God.

Our ability to think requires that we act coherently within a comprehensive perspective with its categorial system. The perspective itself is a matter that we must make a decision about, a radical decision of faith. And on that ultimate level, reason is impotent to determine which perspective is true. That is because the options are ultimates and there is no further standard or norm by which they can be assessed. There is no logical move we can make that will achieve an ultimate premise which is beyond doubt.

We are finally faced with the ultimate choice of a framework which itself will ground all our subsequent ultimate choices and give them meaning within the order of reality. This ultimate choice, the venture of faith, is like no other choice in human experience. And the knowledge of faith, although clearly knowledge, is like no other knowledge. Faith and the core beliefs of faith are a unique form of knowledge, ultimate knowledge, knowledge as surrender, knowledge as gift.

Therefore, no matter how valid our reasons are, no matter how much others ought to accept them, they need only be accepted as compelling by others when others share the categorial system in terms of which the reasons are compelling. When the discussion revolves around reasons for accepting this and not that as the ultimate source and ground for life, the reasons will be accepted by others only when they surrender to the ultimate which is the ground for the categorial system in terms of which the reasons are compelling.

For these reasons, I conclude that although reasons may be the medium to faith, they cannot establish ultimate certainty and cannot be the final ground for my faith. They can negatively ensure that my actions are not inappropriate to my basic commitment.

I affirm with Pinnock that God "can surely use the evidences of his activity and existence to effect the conversion of the human heart." My point is that without surrender to God in faith, a person will "resist them" and not accept them as compelling for him or her. The reality of resistance (sin) is, of course, no excuse. And the importance of surrender in the acceptance of reasons ought never to lead to smugness, but to increased activity in presenting the claims of the Gospel with all the logic, pedagogy, style, and empathy at our disposal.

Faith is faith
Does all this mean that for me, as Pinnock and Bloesch fear, faith is irrational? By no means. Is faith then rational for me? It is not. Faith is faith, and the debate about the rationality or irrationality of faith is, I suggest, wrong-headed from the start.

In my understanding, all human acts are multi-dimensional unities involving thinking and all the other human ways of being. They differ in kind — according to the way of being which qualifies and dominates the activity. Thus, for example, troth-acts such as parenting and marrying are qualified by troth, with all the other ways of being subsumed to troth; economic acts of buying and selling are qualified by stewardship, with all the other ways subsumed. Faith-acts such as praying, confessing, and worshipping are qualified by faith, with all the other ways subsumed, including the rational.

When we distinguish in this way between different *ways* of being (which are unique and irreducible) and *acts* (which include all the ways of being in differing configurations), it becomes apparent that an *act* of faith can be rational or irrational even though faith as such is other than and different from rationality. In the same way an act of troth can be rational or irrational even though troth itself is other than and different from rationality. In this way I am also able to discuss the place of reason in coming to faith and the effect of reasons or the lack of them on faith life without making faith itself rational or irrational.

Avoiding dogmatism and relativism

The Bible has a "discrimen" for interpretation and it alone should be ours. I could not agree more with Pinnock and Carl Henry. My point, which Pinnock does not seem to take seriously enough, is that we have to recognize that our appropriation of the biblical discrimen is *our* appropriation and therefore approximate, partial, fallible, and time-conditioned. Dogmatism, I am arguing, ill becomes the Christian church.

Does this mean, as Pinnock suggests, that I am flirting with a relativistic one-view-is-as-good-as-another view? It does not. The differing views of biblical authority need to be tested and compared in order to choose the one which provides, in our view, the best access to the scriptural message.

The most difficult and important task facing the Christian church is navigating a passage between the rationalistic rocks of dogmatism and the irrationalist eddies of relativism. So to navigate is my intent.

On the one hand, to talk about the biblical message as if our interpretation of it is independent of our own viewpoint is the pretense of dogmatism. It makes the Bible captive to our own prejudices. And then we are truly blind. On the other hand, to talk about the biblical message as if any interpretation of it is as valid as any other is the delusion of relativism. It too makes the Bible captive to our own prejudices. And then we are truly empty.

For our encouragement

Indeed, it is to avoid violation of the biblical text that I suggest we need to pay attention to the structural specificity of the Bible as a text to engender, encourage, and orient faith. That is in fact what the Scriptures say about themselves: "For all the ancient Scriptures were written for our own instruction, that we through encouragement and comfort of Scriptures might have hope" (Rom. 15:4; also I Cor. 10:1, John 20:21, Heb. 13:22). How that is a "skewing" of the text is difficult for me to understand. Of course, if it can be shown that my proposal distorts or obscures the text, so much the worse for my proposal.

For me, "certitudinal" is a handy designation for the kind of text the Scriptures are, a book exhorting its readers about the ultimate certitudes of life. This distinguishes it from other kinds of texts, such as telephone books, do-it-yourself manuals, or economic treatises, and puts it in a unique class with other "sacred" writings. Knowing that the Scriptures are approaching all of life from the angle of ultimate certainty and the total surrender of faith helps orient me to hear its abiding message, its enduring claim, and its abundant hope even as I read about people and situations far removed from my own.

In interpretation approach is everything. Just as wrong questions lead to useless answers, so wrong approaches cause frustration, confusion, and violation. A certitudinal hermeneutic does not narrow the Bible's purpose nor hollow out its content. Its concern is with achieving the proper approach to the textual content in order that misunderstandings be averted. It wants to tune readers to the proper frequency so that we will be attuned to the biblical message and hear it with a minimum of static and interference.

It is in that connection that I warn against approaching the Scriptures as if they were *merely* books of information or propositional depositories. Books of information may or may not be helpful; propositions may or may not be true. However, certitudinal discourse (which includes information, stories, history, propositions, etc., as the case may be) announces itself as truth which commands acceptance and committed action. It is not that I deny, as Pinnock says, the propositional content of Scripture. But considering only the Scriptures' propositions is a reductionist view which misses the unique character of Scripture as claim and promise.

Certitudinal hermeneutics is not vague (contrary to Pinnock), but neither does it predetermine the content of the exegesis (which Bloesch applauds). As any method, it can do only so much, and as any method, it can be misused. What it does do is arm us with an awareness that the text's abiding message will, whatever the details, address us fundamentally on the certitudinal level. Since faith is the motivator and integrator of all human activities, via the faith focus, the text will claim all of our lives.

The abiding message to be heard is not first of all moral, political, economic, emotional, logical or whatever; even though it will have cognitive content, evoke emotional response, and have moral, political, and economic implications. Even moral precepts such as "husbands love your wives" are misread when primarily or exclusively read morally. That becomes exceedingly clear when attention is paid to the phrase "in the Lord" which in Ephesians and Colossians is part of the sanctions. Loving one's wife is, of course, the right, expected, and proper thing to do. Paul, however, gives the moral responsibility its ultimate ground and force by insisting that it be done "in the Lord." If we fail to hear that, we have tuned out the central thrust of the message.

However, the certitudinal focus of the Biblical teaching does not, as I have argued in my paper, take away from its normative bearing on all of our decisions and actions, whatever their nature or stripe. Rather than limiting its normative force, the certitudinal focus describes and specifies the way Scripture works out its abiding normativity for all of life. Exegetically, Scripture invites us to come to every text with our ultimate, life-and-death questions, to hear its abiding, life-giving message, to be sensitive to the abiding, life-enhancing norms which it offers or to which it witnesses, and, in response, to form and inform all the rules we make, all the decisions we take, and all the actions we enact, guided by these norms, loyal to that vision, faithful to the Spirit.[1]

If, as I suggest, the ultimate intention of Scripture is to encourage and challenge us in the faith, on that level Scripture asks to be read literally. Thus, when Matt. 5:34 tells us that our heavenly Father feeds the birds of the air, we are to take that as literally true. We need not, faced with our observations about the food supply of birds, discount these words as only figurative. They are, when all is said and done, the full and final conclusion that needs to be accepted literally as true. Birds, too, live and move and have their being by the grace and power of the Creator God.

I have found it helpful to think, in this connection, of a birth announcement which proud parents often send to their friends and acquaintances. "God gave us a daughter" is not hyperbole or myth nor does it call into question their role as parents nor does it ignore all the other dimensions of the event (the weight, length, and name of the baby are duly recorded, as well as the place and time). But it announces that the story of human birth is incomplete until it is recognized and acknowledged that children are gifts from the hand of God, gifts which we receive in the course of living responsibly as human creatures of God.

Such depth-level meaning which either elicits surrender to its truth or encounters deep resistance characterizes the Scripture as a whole. Since examples serve to clarify and since the worth of my approach will be judged by whether it does facilitate consistent and edifying interpretations, permit me an example or two.

Debt-free
Recently I heard of a conscientious Christian couple who in

their reading of Rom. 13:8 "Owe no person anything" felt constrained to sell their house in order to liquidate their mortgage and be debt-free. Now they rent. Is this what God demands of all of us? Are all of us who hold mortgages disobedient, not trusting that God will take care of us?

Some say such a demand is ridiculous and impossible today. Others accept that the norm is clear, Christians ought to be debt-free, but in a fallen world it is impossible to live by the Christian ethic. Some learn to live with that schizophrenia, with or without guilty consciences.

A certitudinal approach, in my view, offers a coherent, consistent reading which, neither defusing the text as figurative nor declaring it a moral ideal, takes it literally on the ultimate level of faith as truth. To begin with, employing the method, we anticipate that the text will be fundamentally addressing us on the ultimate faith level of human existence, regardless of its immediate focus or content.

In that anticipation, "owe no man anything," seen in context with its following phrase "except to love one another," does not first of all have a specific economic meaning. It means that we are to fulfill all our obligations to each other, loving God, neighbor and self. Then we have done everything that God commands and we owe no one anything.

From that level, its meaning stretches out to all the nooks and crannies of our existence, including our pocketbooks. We ought not to over-extend ourselves economically, nor ought we to deprive fellow humans of their economic livelihood. That does not belong to service of God and neighbor.

Obeying Romans 13:8, it turns out, is not as easy (or misguided) as selling our houses. Only after taking in its faith-meaning are we able to search out its meaning for us today in all the areas of life.

Gold and pearls
I Timothy 2:9 prohibits women from having braided hair and from wearing gold, pearls, and expensive clothes. Some Christians take this as an explicit dress-code for women. Most of us prefer to ignore it with some reference to the cultural situation of the day. Both approaches, in my view, are too easy and miss the thrust of the text.

Anticipating that the text will have a certitudinal thrust, we notice the emphasis in the context on "modesty and soberness" and on "good works proper for women who profess to be religious."

Now the central meaning becomes clear. Christian women ought to be adorned in ways fitting their confession. In the situation at hand, Paul judges that this means not being decked out in pearls and costly array, as presumably the prostitutes were. What about today? The text does not specify, but it does forthrightly challenge all of us to relate our adornment and fashions to our faith and to get our priorities straight. Unless we address that question, we have not heard the message of the text.

No thought

Or take Matthew 6:25: "Take no thought for your life, what you shall eat or what you shall drink, or for your body what you shall put on." Plainly that is a ridiculous text which is impossible to obey. Planning for tomorrow, worry about food and drink and clothes is part of life. In fact, anxiety is not always negative. It often helps us to be better prepared and to avoid disasters. So we try to cut the text down. Don't be overly concerned, we say. But that misses the heartbeat of this text and leaves us feeling guilty when we are anxious.

If, however, we read the text as depth-level truth, we get a wholly different picture of things. In Jesus Christ, through the Spirit of God, we are free from anxiety at the root of our existence. Our natural anxiousness which is part of human life is not bottomless. Our life is hid with Christ in God. We are free from the anxiety of believing that our salvation depends on our ability to keep God's law. Freed from that anxiety, we are free to do God's law, and enabled to seek the welfare of others and the kingdom of God without radical anxiety about ourselves and our needs. That is the surprise of the Kingdom of God.

A developmental, pastoral hermeneutic

In giving a few brief examples I do not mean to suggest that only with an explicit certitudinal hermeneutic will one arrive at the conclusions I have suggested. I may have misused the method. And others have arrived at similar conclusions from the biblical text. My concern is for consistency in method, for an exegetical approach which is able to deliver edifying interpretations of Scripture without arbitrariness in selection of data and in method of interpretation. I suggest that a certitudinal approach offers us consistency and perspective in sorting out the abiding principles from the circumstantial and contextual ways in which they are given in Scripture. The changing, on-going nature of the historical process is reflected in the dynamic nature of revelation in

Scripture.[2] Concomitant with an unfolding revelation, we need to be more fully aware of a need for a developmental hermeneutic. Just as the later prophets re-envision, re-interpret, and re-apply the words of the Torah and the former prophets for new situations, just as the four evangelists and the apostles shape their writings to speak directly to the concerns of the people they are addressing, so we are called to re-envision the central thrust of the Scriptural message for our time and day. That is not undermining, rejecting or opposing the message of Scripture, but expressing its significance more fully in ways relevant in new situations.[3] Mandated and led by the Spirit of truth promised in John 16, we may even be led in obedience to Scripture to accept as permissible what specific words of Scripture prohibit. A small but instructive example is provided by returning to I Timothy 2. In most Christian communities the wearing of gold, pearls and expensive clothes by women is no longer considered immodest and intemperate, even though Paul forbids them. At the same time, hearing the abiding message of good works with modesty and sobriety in our day and age of such extremes of poverty and wealth raises in a new way for women — and for men — how our life-style witnesses to or betrays the gospel.

The final goal or standard for the adequacy of the exegesis of Scripture (and all sacred writings) must be its ability to edify and exhort. Scripture is a pastoral book, concerned to feed and shepherd the souls of the faithful. As befits such a book, our interpretive procedures should show an over-riding pastoral concern. Pastoral considerations of comfort and hope, encouragement and admonition, not questions of authorship, historicity or literary form, need to guide our exegesis. If certain ways or methods, no matter how refined or erudite, do not help us hear the Word more clearly, do the Truth more fully, and express Love more deeply, they need to be revised or rejected. Even when due attention is paid to matters of genre, audience, context, language, kind of text, history, and pre-understandings, any interpretation of Scripture which does not build the faith is misleading and inadequate. At the same time — to avoid misunderstanding on this cardinal point — let me affirm again that proper attention to all these matters remains indispensable: the normal route to an edifying interpretation is via proper attention to the full realities of text and interpreter(s) in their complex interaction. Here my point is that without conscious and continual awareness of their pastoral intent, our exegetical procedures will serve up stones rather than bread.

Bible and philosophy

One of Pinnock's more pressing concerns is what he perceives to be the magisterial operation of Dooyeweerd's thinking which gives the Bible the "place that system permits it to have." That is a serious objection, particularly since I intend the opposite.

The involved question of the relation of philosophy to hermeneutic theory and theology in general needs much more attention. In this context I will have to limit myself to a brief comment.

Interpreting the Bible is a human endeavor which necessarily makes use of human categories. So the choice is not between a "pure" understanding of the text and one that uses human philosophical categories. The problem is to find the "right" philosophical categories, categories which do not obscure and distort biblical revelation.

The fact that I use Dooyeweerd, that Bultmann used Heidegger, that Thomas used Aristotle is, thus, not the exception that Pinnock suggests. Willy-nilly, consciously or unconsciously, every theologian and every exegete uses somebody's categorial system. Indeed a "pure," "presuppositionless" approach to Scripture is itself indebted to the *tabula rasa* empiricistic approach of John Locke. Much work remains to be done in comparing and testing the categories we use as we search for the categories which best allow the Bible to speak as it intends to speak.

Conceiving of the Scriptures as a certitudinally qualified book helps me to do more justice to the complex phenomena of Scripture itself. There is widespread agreement that Scripture is neither an encyclopedia nor a scientific textbook. Attempts to treat the Scriptures as handbooks for morality, etiquette, politics, business, or counselling are highly selective pick-and-choose endeavors which not only tend to ignore matters of context but disregard much if not most of the scriptural text. In this situation many thinkers are emphasizing that the intention of the biblical material "is religious rather than, say, historical or scientific."[4]

However, since "religious" means for many non-natural or supernatural, the urgent question remains as to *how* a "religious" book speaks to natural life, history and science. Perhaps, as some conclude, it has nothing to say for ordinary human life and history.

It is in addressing this issue of *how* a "religious" book functions with authority in all of life that I have found very helpful Dooyeweerd's idea that faith is one natural mode of being human which plays a leading and integrative role in relation to all the other ways of being human. For when I approach the Scriptures with the notion that their over-riding focus — whatever the literary genre, whatever the historical context — is on ultimate certitude, I find myself able to bring into sharper relief the integral unity of Scripture in its dynamic diversity. Focussing on the guiding and integrative role which the certitude of faith plays in its inter-relation with all the other ways of being in the world also opens up for me in deeper ways how a book structured certitudinally is able to exercise abiding — guiding and integrative — authority in relation to all these other ways of being in the world. Rather than obscuring or distorting Scripture, awareness of Scripture's certitudinal focus helps me honor the text as it presents itself and attunes me to hear more sensitively its abiding message as I re-envision it for today.

My approach — or something like it — is needed to help us honor the divine authority of Scripture without playing down or romanticizing its creatureliness. Rather than giving the Bible "its place," my proposal, by honoring the phenomena of Scripture, intends to place itself in service of Scripture, in order that the Bible can be for us an instrument of liberation from the bonds of our own perspectives.

Faithful vs objective exegesis

Pinnock is also puzzled by my denial of both the possibility and desirability of the "objective" exegesis of Scripture. Part of the problem, at least in this case, is semantic. I prefer to call an exegesis which does justice to the integrity of the text a "faithful" exegesis.

My problem with so-called objective exegesis is that no exegesis is or can be freed from the subjectivity of the interpreter. Talk of "objective" exegesis tries to hide this reality. In fact, "objective exegesis" puts the control in the hands of the operator who is to secure the meaning of the text through rigorous application of methods. Hidden in this arrangement and its methods is an unwarranted faith in the autonomy of human reason. Such methodological positivism is essentially no less subjectivistic than existentialism. Both need to be avoided.

This also gives me occasion to emphasize again the pivotal place of pre-understandings. Bloesch has a rather negative view of them, preferring that we come to Scripture without any overt presuppositions. I suggest that the more we are aware of the pre-understandings that we bring to the text, the more it is possible to avoid making the "text conform to *a priori* speculation." It's precisely when we are unaware of our pre-understandings that we are most in danger of imposing on the text. "After all, we came to the text clean!"

Form and content
Although Donald Bloesch's response to my proposal is generally positive, he does have some concerns. Since I do not see myself in basic disagreement with Bloesch on any of these points, I trust that my brief comments will serve to deepen our dialogue. Indeed, for me the "vision of the text" is the biblical message, what I also refer to as the certitudinal thrust of the text. It is not the particular world-view of the author of the text or his emotional state or his economic situation.

Is my hermeneutic too dependent on existentialist thought? That is up to others, of course, to judge. Let me just say that I have learned from existentialist thinkers. However, in terms of hermeneutics, as my essay indicates, I have learned more from thinkers such as Polanyi, Gadamer and Ricoeur who themselves have trenchant criticisms of existentialism (which I share) and want to move beyond its extreme subjectivism. Moreover, at crucial points I have availed myself of the work of Herman Dooyeweerd, who is certainly no existentialist. The fundamental intention of Scripture is to lead to a saving knowledge of Jesus Christ, as Bloesch indicates, and I would add, to a life of service to God and neighbor. That is expressing the intention in terms of message and content. To say that an aim of the text is to transform the self-understanding of the interpreter (which certainly includes transforming our view of God, humanity and the world) in no way takes away from what Bloesch suggests. Rather, it is to describe the intention in terms of its *formal* intention.

I need to emphasize that describing Scripture in terms of its redemptive-reconciling content does not clash with a formal, structural description. In most of his comments Bloesch plays one off against the other. For example, when I talk of the hermeneutic task as a delineation of the message or vision fixed in the text, he asks whether the hermeneutic task is not the "discerning of the Spirit's intention as he speaks to us through the text." But the two are not in conflict. We set out to discern the Spirit's intention by delineating the message of the text.

Another example: I describe the governing focus of the Scriptures formally and structurally as concern with "the ultimate questions of life and death." Bloesch sees the central focus of Scripture as the "proclamation of God's act of reconciliation and redemption in Jesus Christ." But again the two are not in conflict.

My concern is to point out that, formally speaking, Scripture presents its message and addresses its subject-matter from a certain point of view, i.e., ultimacy and final certitude. The answer the Scripture presents, from its certitudinal point of view, is the Gospel of Grace.

A third example: Bloesch sees Jesus Christ as the "spectacles" by which we make sense of life; I describe a vision of life as the "spectacles" through which we make a sense of life. In a biblically-attuned vision of life, Jesus will have a central place. It is through such a vision that we work out in daily experience what it means to find renewal of life in the spirit of Christ.

Word-of-God-for-creation
There is one area where it appears that Bloesch and I may disagree. To me it seems that Bloesch lacks sufficient appreciation for general revelation. I see the biblical emphasis on Jesus Christ as mediator of redemption in terms of the Johannine and Pauline emphasis on the Word as the mediator of creation. In that light, all of creation is revelatory of the Word of God. Sin blinds us to that revelation and distorts it, but it does not destroy it. In Christ, according to the redemptive revelation in Scripture, we can again see the Word of God and be directed by it.

Giving due place to the Word of God for creation can also make us aware that "the bridge which spans the wide chasm between biblical salvation history and contemporary history" is not language or history or the history of the people of God (Braaten) but the creating and sustaining Word of God (cf. II Peter 3:5-7). It is according to the Word of God for creation that the Spirit of God, in the Incarnate Word, renews creation and dwells within but also acts upon the People of God.

Scriptural texts
My reply will not be complete without a short response to Gerald Sheppard. In the first place I confess that I feel at home in the scenario that he paints. I sense that he understands not only my proposal, but its roots, motivations and intentions. For this I am both encouraged and thankful, all the more so because his response is so positive and enthusiastic.

At the same time, Sheppard wants more exegetical detail and more conversation with significant secondary literature in biblical studies. He raises legitimate concerns. I am only too conscious of the need to test the method in detailed exegesis. For if the method does not help in interpretation, so much for the method. At the same time, before we can test a method, we need to be introduced to it in its various features. Now — since the proposal has been made — is the time for thorough testing. I especially invite biblical scholars to test out my approach. Here, as a philosophical theologian, I especially need the help of colleagues in biblical studies. It is in this context that I particularly appreciate that Sheppard, himself an Old Testament scholar, is very positive about my hermeneutic proposal.

I do want to make brief comments on two other matters that Sheppard raises. He prefers to talk of "scriptural texts" rather than "certitudinal texts." Since my major concern is that "sacred texts" be recognized as a distinct type of literature, I am less concerned about the technical terms we employ to designate their distinctness. I have no problem talking about "scriptural texts." At the same time, I am suggesting that a "more rigorous specification" of "scriptural texts" involves notice of their preoccupation with and focus on matters of "ultimate certitude."

Sheppard also wants to distinguish between revelation as "a universal principle of human existence" and the "more historically specific claim that God through the power of the Holy Spirit has revealed something about Scripture to us." So do I. But I do not set the former over against the latter. In my understanding, the Christian claim about Scripture is a unique historical instantiation of revelation as a creational universal. I understand Sheppard to be saying the same thing when he talks of relating the "existential requirement of some 'faith' in order to live in the world" to revelation by the Holy Spirit concerning Scripture. In my understanding, there is an existential requirement of some "revelation" — corresponding to some "faith" — in order to live in the world. In terms of this universal, revelatory dynamic, we can begin to understand the similarities and distinctness when biblical revelation is compared to the nature and forms of revelation in other faiths.

In conclusion, let me note that I fully share with Bloesch — and I am sure with Pinnock and Sheppard — a belief that the Word of God is never at our disposal. At the most fundamental level, we do not "possess" the Word, the Word has us in its "grip." Hermeneutic dexterity does not guarantee a hearing of the Word. But in God's design, as part of working out our salvation with fear and trembling, we are called to a proper use of Scripture. We are to develop a method of interpretation which is pastoral, i.e., appropriate to the redemptive-edificatory purpose of Scripture. It is my hope that we will continue and extend our discussions.

NOTES

1. Allen Verhey has recently written a fine book, *The Great Reversal: Ethics and the New Testament* (Grand Rapids: Eerdmans, 1984), in which he, after establishing that the New Testament presents no unitary ethic, cogently and candidly — and I believe rightly — argues that it is inappropriate to Scripture to ask questions on the "moral-rule level." "To ask Scripture to be what it is not is inappropriate; therefore, to ask it to be a systematic treatise or a comprehensive code or an autonomous ethic based on reason alone is inappropriate" (p. 175). Verhey argues that it is legitimate to ask questions of Scripture on the "ethical-principle" level, although even here we must be careful because we will not find "some autonomous principle or principles, impartial to commitments and loyalties, and resting on reason alone" (p. 177). It is questions of "identity and integrity," "loyalties and commitments" at the "post-ethical" level — what I call the certitudinal level — that Scripture most directly answers. It is answers to these questions — what I have called ultimate, certitudinal questions — which form and inform dispositions and intentions on the "ethical-principle" level which in turn form and inform decisions and judgments at the "moral-rule" level (pp. 176-77).

2. In chapter three of his *The Inspiration of Scripture; Problems and Proposals* (Philadelphia: Westminster Press, 1980), Paul J. Achtemeier has helpfully summarized "how the evidence presented by Scripture itself, the so-called 'phenomena,' points to an explanation of Scripture as a process in which traditions are formulated and reformulated, interpreted and reinterpreted" (pp. 76-94). Cf. also Clark Pinnock's discussion in his recent book, *The Scripture Principle* (San Francisco: Harper & Row, 1984), ch. 8, "Unfolding Revelation," pp. 175-197.

3. Richard N. Longenecker has begun to work out a developmental hermeneutic in splendid fashion in reference to Galations 3:28 in his *New Testament Social Ethics for Today* (Grand Rapids: Eerdmans, 1984).

4. Achtemeier, *op. cit.*, p. 147. Cf. also, G. C. Berkouwer, *Holy Scripture* (Grand Rapids: Eerdmans, 1975), p. 140.